You're Not Allowed to Shoot Me!

A Dutch Family's WWII Survival Story

Dear Juor,

Treasured memories of my family
and myself in peace and war time
It is such a pleasure to work
with your daughter Emily.

Warm regards
Jochebed

by Jochebed Katan

with the assistance of Rachel McRae

You're Not Allowed to Shoot Me

Author: Jochebed Katan

jkatan.book@gmail.com

Copyright © 2014

ISBN: 978-0-9939121-0-8

Published by: Royal George Publishing

Printed and Designed by: Allan Graphics Ltd., Kingston, Ontario

www.allangraphics.ca

TABLE OF CONTENTS

ACKNOWLEDGEMENTS

When I was a young child, my mother told me stories about the past. After my father died, it became very important to me to preserve the history in those stories. Over twenty years, I set about gathering all the information about my parents' lives, encouraging my mother to audiotape her memories, and organizing boxes of documents, photographs, letters and artifacts. These recordings and items formed the foundation of what has become this book, all of which I translated from Dutch. However, on my own I could never have achieved this.

Above all others, this book could not have been completed without the help of Rachel McRae, my primary editor. When we first started working together, we were just trying to make sense of the huge pile of material I had collected. My first question to Rachel was, "How can I preserve all of this history?" She told me to start translating the stories from the tapes my mother left me from Dutch into English and then send them to her. She then edited and correlated these translations into a chronological sequence. While this was happening, I was busily archiving all of the photos, documents and other materials I had, and from this emerged yet more stories. In order to preserve so many tales from the past, Rachel advised that a book seemed the most sensible solution. Because of the distance between our homes, we used the internet to work side-by-side to slowly build this manuscript. Rachel edited all my notes full of stories and shaped them into an enjoyable read. While Rachel researched and wrote contextual historical information, I chose from the extensive collection of photographs and artifacts. All those were important for illustrating what would become this book, and Rachel converted them to electronic form. Although it was a great deal of work, carried out over two years, we both approached it happily, contentedly, and enthusiastically. Without Rachel, this book would never have been possible. I want to thank her for the commitment and love she has shown for this project. Thank you dearly, Rachel, for helping me preserve my mother's memories.

After my immigration to Canada, I showed the materials I had from Holland to Gerald Tulchinsky, a history professor at Queen's University, who urged me to write a book. Although I was not ready to do this at that time, he was the first one to open my eyes to this possibility. Thank you, Gerald, for planting that seed and, twenty years later, writing the foreword for this book!

During hikes in the countryside around Kingston, I discussed with my dearest late friend Bernie Adell, Professor Emeritus Faculty of Law in Queens' University, and professional editor of law journals, the idea of publishing my mother's memoirs. Over time, he gave me much sound advice on the shaping of the book, drawing on his extensive experience. Thank you, Bernie, for taking the time to edit many successive drafts of the book and for all your endless support throughout this entire journey.

I received lots of support and encouragement from members of my family. My daughter Marjoleine de Wild has supported me from the beginning to the end with lots of interest and suggestions. And my son Hajo Schimmelpenningh did a lot of scanning for me; thank you for your time.

My sister Hedie Katan has pushed very hard for a written book, and she wants to see it made into a movie one day. Martijn Katan, my first cousin, showed me lots of pictures from his side of the family, from before and after the war. He provided valuable information about his parents, Richard and Roosje Katan, grandmother Judikje Katan-Sanders, and aunt Eva Katan. This has now become a chapter in this book.

I received huge support for writing this book from René van Wijngaarden, a distant relative of mine. As I provided him with van Daelen information for his book, Engraved in the Palm of my Hands, he has provided me with information for my book.

Flip, Peter, Dik and Aad Went, my dear Went brothers, all of whom are still living: I would like to thank you dearly for all the stories you have told me over time, and the love you gave me as a young child.

Even though I had never met him before starting this book, Lisa van de Bunt, the son of my father's employer, became not just a great source of information but also a friend. Thank you, Lisa, for bringing me back to the old Went house where I lived during the war.

In doing research for this book, I met with Corrie van Seijen for the first time in many years. Corrie gave me lots of information about her father, Jan van Seijen, who suffered greatly for hiding my parents. Thank you, Corrie, for your warmth and kindness.

Throughout the writing of this book, I always had the help of wonderful students from Queen's University: Shanee Honig, Zoe Joffe, Ben Carver, and Emily Gottschalk. Because all of my materials are spoken or written in Dutch, having English-speaking helpers always with me was very important. They obtained many books from the Queen's University library for me to be used for research. With all of them, I had a warm relationship, and I want to thank them for their time, input, and energy. Without all of you, I could not have written this book.

To my friend, Jane Rodgers, I am very appreciative for all her final editing with the "red pen." Your advice was always welcome and effective.

I am also grateful to Rachel's friends, Richard Ascough, Director of the Queen's School of Religion, and Mary-Lynne

Ascough, former editor at McGill-Queen's Press, for their excellent advice and editing suggestions, and also to Joan MacKinnon for designing the family trees that appear in this book.

I would like to thank Dan Graham and Bryan Babcock of Allan Graphics for their excellent job of designing and printing this volume.

And most importantly, this book could not have been written without my mother, Rie Katan-van Daelen. The clarity of her memories of people, places, and events was incredible. She preserved all memorabilia as evidence of what happened to our family. As well, she had a natural gift for storytelling, which gives the book its energy. It is with profound gratitude to her that I am publishing her stories.

Jochebed Katan

PREFACE

Of the 140,000 Jews living in the Netherlands on the eve of the German conquest in May of 1940, only about 15-20,000 survived the war. The rest were put to death on native ground or murdered at Sobibor and Auschwitz. This was a casualty rate of 85 percent, similar to that of Poland, the worst of the Holocaust of European Jewry, and it was carried out with the same efficiency and commitment as was employed in the Reich itself.

Jews in the Netherlands, the historian Raul Hilberg points out, were especially vulnerable because of their living in a country with no easily accessible natural escape routes, bounded as it was by Germany, the North sea, and Belgium. Except for a tiny few who managed to get away in time, Jews were trapped.

As well, the German administration in occupied Holland was headed by Reichkommissar Seyss-Inquart, a zealous Austrian who was assisted by a group of fellow Austrians, some with experience in "handling" minorities in their home country. They exercised power with "utter ruthlessness and efficiency" on their own initiative without instructions from Berlin. They were able to rely on the efficient and compliant civil service, the police force, numerous collaborators, and the Jewish Council, 'de Joodse Raad'. As it is so graphically portrayed in this remarkable memoir, the Holocaust then proceeded methodically through its five stages: definition, expropriation, concentration, deportation, and destruction.

First, came the definition of who was a Jew. Since the Nuremberg Laws in September 1935, this was a significant issue in Western European countries conquered by Germany because of the large number of mischling (half and quarter Jews), of whom there were at least 20,000 – some estimates ran as high as 300,000 – in the Netherlands. Persons married to Jews or those who followed the Jewish religion were defined as Jews and, therefore, automatically victims.

The second stage, expropriation, followed quickly. This entailed wholesale dismissal from employment and curtailment of opportunities for Jews in the professions, and the seizure of businesses, bank accounts, insurance policies, residences, and personal property of all kinds. These rigorously applied actions, which were assisted by major German banks, resulted in the looting of hundreds of millions of guilders and the complete impoverishment of the Jewish community.

Next came the concentration of Jews in an ever-tightening structure of identification and movement controls, making it easy for authorities to identify and round up victims. The Joodse Raad officials felt forced to accede to German directives, notably those dealing with deportations, the fourth stage of the Holocaust, which began in June 1942.

Jews were to present themselves in designated groups – some were composed of unaccompanied children – for transport to "work camps" on pain of severe punishment. They were moved to the transit camps Westerbork and Vught in Holland, which had a combined capacity of 40,000 persons. From there, trains carried the victims to the gas chambers at Sobibor and Auschwitz in occupied Poland for immediate murder.

By the end of the war, the deportations had included:

Mauthausen	1,750
Various concentration camps	350
Auschwitz	60,000
Sobibor	34,300
Theresienstadt	4,900
Bergen Belsen	3,750

Destruction was the final stage of the Holocaust. The process continued apace with relentless efficiency as Seyss-Inquart and his "willing executioners" insisted that quotas had to be complete and that the trains must move on time. He succeeded in destroying the Jews of the Netherlands: by the end of 1944 there were few of them left alive.

Jochebed Katan and her parents miraculously survived the war with the aid of non-Jewish helpers, although with the legacy of extreme pain evident in this account. It is a most moving testament to the suffering that they bore during those years and for the rest of their lives, to the human decency of some strangers and the extreme cruelty of others, and to the almost incredible survival of the human spirit.

February, 2013
Gerald Tulchinsky, Professor Emeritus
Department of History, Queen's University, Kingston, Ontario

Jochebed Katan

The Netherlands during World War II

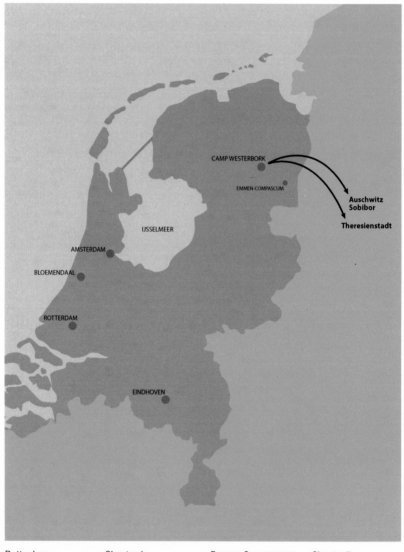

Amsterdam 1940-1941

Happy Times

PART 1

"My name is Jochebed Katan, and I am the author of this book. Since birth, I have had several other names: Jeantje, Julie, Anneke, and Joché. The reason I had so many names is that as a young child, I had to be hidden. Of the six million Jews killed during the Holocaust, 1.5 million were children. Less than one in ten survived, hidden and sheltered by kind strangers. These were extraordinary acts of human dignity. The only way for Jewish parents to escape into hiding was to be separated from their children. This was a terrible deed to do, but they were desperate, and it was the only way to keep their children alive. My parents understood this as well. It was very dangerous for someone to choose to protect and hide a Jew – in 1942 a law was decreed that anyone who helped a Jew to hide would be shot or sent to a concentration camp. Only a small minority had the courage to act. In the midst of evil, they showed humanity at its best.

The Went family, with their six children, took a big risk by taking me into their home. I had possibly the best years of my young childhood while I was in hiding with that family. Of course, I do not remember this time, since I was just a baby when it started.

The stories in this book have mostly come from my mother, Marie Katan-van Daelen, who is always called Rie. When Rie was 88 years old I interviewed her and recorded on audiotape telling her story. She spoke from memory and referenced parts of her past that she had written in preparation for taping. There are 9 tapes of Rie speaking and together they are 3 hours and 37 minutes. She expressed during the interview that she felt it was now time to share everything with her children and her grandchildren for the first time.

Throughout the text there are Author's notes that explain the history, providing background information.

Unless otherwise noted, all of the stories and text in this book are written in Rie's voice. Sometimes, a story comes from another person who was part of those events, and in such cases a special note will be made of who is telling that story."

Rie's Special Birthday

Today is my 82nd Birthday. It is August 1997, and I am in Copenhagen with my children and grandchildren. I am ready now—ready to make my speech. It is a speech that is important to me—important because I want them all to remember my family.

You see here a photo of the van Daelen's oil factory in Rotterdam. It was taken years ago, well before the war, as you can see from the old-fashioned car.

1935-36 - In the Delftse Straat in Rotterdam. Oil barrels from the van Daelen Company.

My grandfather and his cousin started the factory, mixing thinner and thicker quality oils. At first, the factory was very small. The oils were used for machinery—for instance, for the machinery in shoe factories or for wheels for carts. They also made wax and various technical oils.

My grandfather had four sons and they all worked in the family business. That means they all had a car and travelled throughout the entire countryside to sell their products. They were very successful. My father looked after the southern

Hendrik van Daelen wearing a watch chain with the golden barrel. The barrel was given to the owners in 1918 at the 40th anniversary of the factory.

January 1927. Hendrik van Daelen in his office.

part of Holland; he was a very good talker, a real businessman, and in time, his clients became great friends. Uncle Ies stayed at the office—he was the bookkeeper. When my brothers grew up, however, they did not plan to continue in this firm. They started a new company, "the Gebroeders (brothers) van Daelen" and gave the company the name "Harrison" (son of Hendrik, my father).

15 March 1933 - The owners of the van Daelen & van Wessel firm gathered for the 40th anniversary of the firm.

Information about the firm that was printed at that time, including the following: "Over time, the firm has developed improved quality mineral oils and technical greases for industry and nautical purposes, and also better automotive oils."

Jubileum Fa. Van Daelen & Van Wessel Rotterdam.

Op 15 Maart j.l. herdacht de Fa. Van Daelen & Van Wessel, chemisch techn. olie- en vetfabriek te Rotterdam, den dag, waarop zij voor 40 jaar, door de Heeren S. van Daelen & S. van Wessel werd opgericht.

De Firma, die thans door de zoons van den eerstgenoemden wordt voortgezet, heeft zich in den loop der jaren, op het gebied van minerale smeeroliën en technische vetten voor industrie en scheepvaart en betere automobieloliën, toegelegd.

Op bescheiden voet begonnen, heeft zij zich door de energie en activiteit harer firmanten voortdurend uitgebreid en beschikt zij thans over een bekwame staf medewerkers, die trachten de zaak tot verderen bloei te brengen:

They were there until the Germans came. Those despicable men took everything over, and the day came when my brothers were forced to leave their business without one penny of compensation. It was over.

As all mature men did at the time, the men in my family wore a gold chain, which hung from one side of their jacket and across to the opposite pocket. In the middle was a little signet, which was the symbol of their factory. It was a gold oil barrel. The only one I found after the war had been my father's. It was made to commemorate the 25th year of the factory. Good friends of ours had kept this little oil barrel during the war, along with other things for me, and that made me very happy.

On this special day, when we are all here, I would like to give all the ladies a copy of the same barrel on a chain, for you to remember the name van Daelen and the month of August 1997 when I gave it to you. The men will get their barrel in a presse-papier.

It was Jochebed's and Hedie's idea to have these made. I especially thank Hedie for discovering how we could have them made the way I like it. They both kept it a secret, so now I can give them to all of you as a surprise. I hope they will bring nice memories of my 82nd birthday. I also hope we can come together again in the years to come, and that all of us will be in good health.

Ashtray from the office of the firm.

CHAPTER 1

Memories of My Early Life

I was born into the van Daelen family of Rotterdam. My father, Hendrik van Daelen, born in June 1887, was a very dominant man, and my mother, Sara Doodewaard-van Daelen, was always very nervous around him. We had two older brothers. Simon was 2½ years older than us, and Aat (Abraham) was 1½ years older. Then in 1915, along came: identical twins. Our parents named us Jeanne and Marie, but my mother immediately began to shorten my name to Rie. Jeanne was born ten minutes before me, and I was the surprise because my mother didn't know that she was carrying twins. We were very small and were put together in one cradle. I remember her saying that sometimes I licked my sister's toes. She told me that even though she was very

1915 - Rie and Jeanne.

1918 - Aat (Abraham), Jeanne, Rie, Simon van Daelen

1923. Left is Jeanne, right is Rie (in front row). In second year at the public elementary school on Schooterboschstraat 84 in Rotterdam.

busy, it was her easiest birth, because everyone came to help her. My brother Simon said that I was his baby, and it was so until I married.

My sister, Jeanne, and I were identical twins, and we were very close. No one could tell us apart—which was Jeanne and which was Rie? My grandfather and my mother-in-law never could tell the difference. We couldn't do our schoolwork unless we were sitting next to each other. Our mother, a former schoolteacher, was uneasy about this and several times asked the school to separate us. So once, when we were 8 years old, they did separate us. One of us had to sit in the front of the class and one in the back. We couldn't work that way at all, and so, eventually, they put us back together and we could work again.

It was not always so pleasant to be an identical twin. When we were young, we were like little dolls. We hated people looking at us and comparing us, and we especially hated it when they measured us, back to back. When I was 15 or 16, my father asked if one of us would take his film to be developed at the photo shop. I volunteered, and Jeanne said she would go with me. But I refused. I wanted to walk alone on the street, but that had never happened before. Later, I heard my father saying, "Ah, now the twins are beginning to go their separate ways."

My mother was always in favour of us being a bit more separated. It had happened once before when we went to Gerzon, a clothing shop. The manager told my mother that she had two outfits exactly the same for her two girls. I wanted to know what colour they were. "Blue," was the answer. But I said, "If Jeanne chooses the blue one, I'd like to take the pink one." The manager was not pleased because she would have to get the pink outfit from their shop in Amsterdam. But I was adamant, saying quite definitely that I didn't want the same colour as my sister. At that time, I was 13 years old, and although I still wanted to do things with my twin sister, this was the beginning of my own personality. I didn't know it then, nor did I know how different our futures would be.

My brother Aat and I didn't seem to connect. We hardly talked to each other, and there was no love lost between us. We never knew why; perhaps it was because he was more introverted.

Simon was very sweet and never a discipline problem for my mother, while Aat was physically active and always looking for trouble. My brothers went their own way and never bothered with us until we were 16 or 17. Jeanne and I did not play with the boys, only with each other. According to my mother, I was always "the cock of the walk" and bossed Jeanne, who must have suffered a lot as my twin. I did not realize this until much, much later. Once, when we were bridesmaids at our aunt's wedding, my father wrote a song that we were supposed to sing together at the reception. Both of us were always very shy and scared to look adults in the eye. The moment we had to sing, Jeanne was too scared, but I wasn't, so I sang it alone. I was always the last to come home. Simon always said: "Rie arrives home at the same time as the morning paper."

My father dominated the conversation at the dinner table. He was a very good storyteller and became very angry if anyone interrupted him. When I was young, my father was a real dictator. When guests came, it was very cozy, but we children had to be in the other room. He sketched well and bought beautiful paintings. When I grew up, my relationship with my father improved a lot. He was a hardworking, sharp businessman who suffered during the depression, although he always earned good money. Our house was always in prime condition. My father and my brothers worked in the family business, van Daelen & van Wessel, a chemical, technical, oil and grease factory that manufactured industrial lubrication oils. It was located at 269 Insulinde Straat in Rotterdam. The family had enough money to have a comfortable, though not luxurious life. Every year in July or August, our family went on holidays for a month. I remember that we visited Switzerland in 1930 and again in 1937, Paris in 1932, Norway in 1933, and in Antwerp in 1939.

1932 - Family going on holiday. From the left: Hendrik, Sara, Jeanne, Rie, Aat, and Simon van Daelen.

We had a good family life. My mother Sara never worked outside the home—that was not done. She was a housewife. She had been a teacher before she married, and she had a degree in French. She did such fine embroidery that everyone thought it was factory-made. My mother was a very sweet, quiet person. Over the years, my relationship with her got better and better, and I always enjoyed our outings together. In the afternoons my mother took an hour's rest. She had such a lovely down duvet. Every Friday afternoon she baked all afternoon.

We had a two-story house at Proveniersplein 8A in Rotterdam. The downstairs was rented out, but we owned the second and third floor. In those days, my parents had a maid. Maids were very easy to get, and they all said the same thing: that they would be willing to work on condition that they would not have to eat cheap food, like fresh salmon, more than three times a week.

In the dining room there was a little silver bird that hung from the light fixture, which was attached to a bell in the kitchen. When the bell was rung, the maid had to come to clear the dining room table, or serve the meal. That was nothing special - all middle- and upper- class families had such a bell. In the living room, there was one hidden under the carpet so that no one noticed when the maid was called. She ate in the kitchen, and while we were eating our second course, she was already washing the dishes in a basin in the sink. Much later there was a small hot-water tank. Before that, there were always kettles on the stove to warm the water.

At 8:30 in the evening the maid always brought a large, silver hot-water jug to make hot chocolate or tea, along with all kinds of chocolate and cookies. Then she would bring fruit to the table. We all sat around the large table and listened to the radio (TV had not been invented yet). It was always very cozy. On Friday evening we read the newspaper, which was printed on pink paper. Everyone in the house got some pages from it to read until 10 o'clock. Then the boys each made themselves a cup of hot chocolate, and ate sandwiches. Then we all went to bed.

The maid always lived in the house and slept in the attic, where there was a bathroom and storage but no heating. That was customary. The house was heated by two black, shiny, coal stoves, one in the dining room and the other in the living room. Later, they became electric. The living room was not used during the winter, and the pocket doors stayed closed. In the bedrooms, there was no heating. We all had woolen blankets and were sometimes cold, but it was a very expensive time. Later, when we started studying we got a little electric stove on the floor under the big table. We had warm feet, and that was enough for us.

For spring cleaning, an extra cleaning lady always came. The lace curtains had to be washed; they took a great deal of care, as they were made of thin cotton and would tear if not handled carefully when stretched on the drying racks. This was done every year. In our house, there were many smokers: all the men smoked cigars. So the wash water from the curtains looked like coffee. We had nine windows on the front of the house (4+4+1). The curtains inside framed the top of the windows in a canopy, tied back with ribbons. My mother was very proud of these curtains. Later, when I went back in the 1970s, I had tears in my eyes because the second and third floors had been divided into three or four apartments and the beautiful draperies were no longer there.

In my childhood, my mother never went to the shops— everyone came to the door. She kept a list in her little book for the grocer who delivered the groceries the next day. We never did the laundry at home because there was no space. Instead, it was picked up one week and brought back the next. The butcher got his order over the phone, and the milkman, baker, and vegetable and fruit grocer came with horse and wagon to the front door.

My mother used 100 grams of tea and 200 grams of Van Nelle coffee from Rotterdam per week for five people. Coffee was for lunchtime, and my spoiled father always said he got better quality coffee elsewhere. However, coffee was very expensive, and Ma had to manage. We ground the beans in the coffee mill that hung on the wall with a small glazed cup beneath it. When the cup was full, it was just enough for a pot of coffee. Sugar was stored in big round tins that were left over from World War I.

The only place my mother went out to shop was the fish market. She bought, for instance, two enormous gurnards for seven people and paid two-and-a-half guilders. Sometimes, Pa asked what she paid for it, and when she told him, he would exclaim, "Couldn't you get it for a lower price?" But, my mother was not the type for bargaining. The fish was delicious; it was boiled with lemon and breadcrumbs, and served with butter and sauce. That was the only time the big oval pot came to the table. We always ate with fish cutlery and fish plates.

We ate a lot of fried roe and haddock but no cold sliced meat. Delmonte's pilchards were imported from the United States. Salmon was the cheapest fish because it was caught in the local

September 27, 1884 - Hendrik van Daelen (1827-1899) and Suzanne van Wessel (1824-1893).
Rie's Great Grandparents.

canals. When we came home from school, my mother always gave us fried plaice fresh from the pan, but we didn't tell my father about it—it was a secret.

On Friday evenings, we always had a very large chicken, which was carved by my father. Sometimes we had veal stuffed with boiled, spiced, minced meat. It was delicious. Then came dessert in every shape and form. Ma made it every Friday afternoon, and her cakes were always excellent: strawberry, coconut, lemon, apple and so

Simon (1861-1942) and Adriana (1862-1932) van Daelen, Rie's Grandparents.

many other kinds. The prune cake was the most delicious; she used a tool to pit some cherries, which she mixed with strawberries to make a sauce. The cakes were baked first on a coal stove, and since the oven was only warm on one side, the cake had to be turned many times.

When there was a birthday, all the aunts and grandparents came. We made our own ice cream in a special wooden bucket, which had thick layers of ice water with lots of salt. My brother, Aat, had to mix it by turning the handle on the lid. Real cream was mixed in, and then the bucket was put in a blanket, so it could cool and harden. Then, in the evening, at 9 o'clock after tea, everybody enjoyed it.

Jeanne and I were very shy. We cried on the first day of school. Everyone was afraid of one particularly strict teacher. When it was our turn to read, we had to stand up; we always stuttered our way through the reading. She never gave more than a 5 out of 10, even when we did well, because she was afraid that the report card marks would be too high. This was her way of making sure that the examination scores would be high. When she asked the class questions about the lesson, she often skipped my sister and me because we came up with the answers too quickly. She never said anything nice or made us feel comfortable in school. There was lots of homework, and we worked from 7:00 to 9:30 every night. There was school on Saturday mornings until 1:00, four weeks summer vacation, two days off for Easter, two days for Pentecost, and one week for Christmas.

We both walked to school, and when we got older, we biked to school like everyone else in Holland. We had an extremely long and heavy jumping rope, and because I liked turning the skipping rope so much, I did the turning while the entire school took turns jumping one after the other until the bell rang. Jeanne and I were very good at gymnastics. I even got a 10 on my report card because I could long jump the farthest in the entire school. But my father

July, 1914. Sara van Daelen-Doodewaard with son, Aat, 7 ½ weeks old.

1940 - Hendrik van Daelen. Rie's Father.

downplayed it, and said that it was just a side subject. The report cards had to be signed by our father, and he was very angry when we didn't do well. Once, when I was 14, I was caught copying from Jeanne. The teacher took an entire mark off, and I had to stand for half an hour in the corner of the classroom.

We always went to my father's parents, Oma and Opa (Grandma and Grandpa) van Daelen, to show them our report cards. They lived five minutes away, and they would give us candies and a ten-cent coin. With ten cents we could buy multicoloured glazed marbles. Our grandparents were very sweet, warm people. We often gathered at their house for birthdays: one group would be playing bridge and another group would be chatting. It was a close family.

Opa and Oma van Daelen rented a house for a month every year in Scheveningen. Jeanne and I were also allowed to stay there, sometimes. It was close to the beach where there were many enclosed wicker chairs. If you were sitting in one of them, you could not see anything, but you were well protected from the wind.

Opa and Oma would not allow us to swim at the beach; only our feet were allowed in the water. After the beach outing, we were treated to large round waffles with whipped cream: oh, that was so delicious. On Sunday when we walked out to the pier, we were very well dressed with long, white stockings and very nice, white berets. We walked very sweetly holding hands with Oma and Opa. They did not realize that Jeanne and I did not like it at all.

My mother's parents were quite different. My grandfather, Abraham Daniel Doodewaard, died in 1920 when he was quite young, so my grandmother, Adriana Doodewaard-Cohen, was a widow for a long time. She was 78 years old and still very fit when Rotterdam was bombarded in May 1940. She heard the roof collapsing when she was in the basement. She was very big, and she ate the most fatty food. If my mother fried fish, one fish was carried over to my grandmother's. We were never comfortable at her house because there was nothing for us to do.

We were obliged to go there when we had to go to the synagogue. My grandmother was a very severe kind of person. On the odd time when we had to eat there, if we didn't hold the fork the correct way, she slapped our fingers with the handle of the knife. My grandmother had a sister, Aunt Marie, and neither of them was very nice to us. People were very strict with children at that time.

We didn't go to their house very often, as my father was always critical of his in-laws and really kept us away from them. It was never a good atmosphere, but Oma Doodewaard could cook very well, with lots of fat, and we loved that. When my brother Simon got diphtheria, Jeanne and I were not allowed to stay in our house because our parents did not want us infected as well. On the front door was the notice: "Contagious." So we went to Opa and Oma Doodewaard's, and Jeanne and I slept together in one bed that had copper balusters. We cried together a lot, but luckily after four weeks, Simon was better, and we were allowed to go home.

When Jeanne and I were 7 or 8 years old, we were excited because we were invited to a wedding. In the the the synagogue was on Botersloot Street. We sat in the front of the bride's carriage with two horses in front of us; we couldn't see anything, only those massive horses' rumps. It was our responsibility to make sure that the train of the bride's dress was beautifully laid out. The men and women were separated, and we, the little girls, had to stand behind the benches—so again, we saw nothing.

In 1922, when I was 6 years old, the gas lights were changed to electric lights. Gaslight is bluish; electricity is yellow. In the streets, the gaslight people had to reach up to light them with a long stick. Before electricity, hardly anybody went out late at night because it was so dark, but with the new electric lanterns, people started going out in the evenings. Even the shop windows were lit with electricity.

My mother, Sara, had thick black straight hair. But Jeanne and I had the van Daelen hair: thin, straight, and black. At the time, everyone had braids. Our mother was so good to us, and bought us small red ribbons, which we wore very proudly to school. But after half an hour, you could see our teacher already grinning because the ribbons had already fallen out; that sweet lady tried twice to put them back in. When the permanent hair curl was invented, Ma got her hair permed. They cut off the chignon of hair at the back and permed her hair. To perm hair, they put electrical wires through it, but it didn't work for Jeanne and me because our hair was so straight. It was very sad when Ma decided to cut our hair short. In our family, the men quickly went bald, and all the girls had thin, straight hair. Elkan, my future husband, had very thick, curly hair; he was the first one in the family with dark brown, curly hair and no glasses. All the van Daelens had glasses. I got my first pair of glasses when I was 10 years old. I hated them. I was the first one in the class to get glasses, but they worked: they opened up the world for me.

We had problems with shoes, too. We had very tiny feet—the smallest size, 18, was still too big for us. After my 15th birthday, I never grew past a size 2½, and Jeanne was the same. Even at my engagement party, I had no new white shoes. My difficult mother-in-law was not very pleased, but in all Holland, they had none in my size—the smallest size was 3½. I was always very healthy until I got the flu and a boil in my ear, which the doctor punctured. It was very painful, and I had a very high fever. My bed was moved to the other side of the room. Because of the high fever, I had a growth spurt and grew 1 cm. taller than Jeanne. So everybody said, "Now we can see the difference between the two of you."

Jeanne and I may have looked exactly alike, but we were different in abilities. Jeanne was much better in mathematics than me, but she couldn't draw. I was much better in languages. Every time we calculated our report card, we prayed to God that our averages would work out to be the same.

We played lots of sports. We were both always very good in gymnastics. We went to a gymnastics school, where we also got our swimming diplomas. The director of the school personally recommended that we join the swimming club. That was great. Every day after school, we trained in the swimming pool. In 1928, the Olympic Games were held in Amsterdam. Jeanne and I were thirteen years old and totally absorbed by them. We trained for the big meets. We never participated, but the idea of training with the world-famous Zus Braun and Rie Mastenbroek (female swimmers), was something special. Both of them won gold medals in those Games. The very special thing was that my mother, who had never learned to swim, took swimming lessons, and in her 40th year she managed to get a swimming certificate.

We got five cents every day to buy a special type of biscuit after swimming. Once, we went with the entire swimming club to The Hague for a swim meet, and I won three prizes. The third prize was a medallion, but I chose a box of chocolates instead. The girls all teased me about choosing chocolates, but I told them that they were for my mother. I was 14 years old when I gave my mother those chocolates. She was so pleased she blushed.

When we were twelve years old, the boys organized a small tennis club on an inside court. This was the beginning of years and years of tennis pleasure. Jeanne and I became members of a larger club in Rotterdam, and in our free time we played there as well.

My father taught us how to skate. All of us skated behind him on a long rope along the frozen ditches. The entire neighbourhood skated. We had wooden skates with colorful cloths to bind them to our boots, called Doorlopers. Later, the bindings were made of leather.

We biked everywhere. My father's first car was a Model T Ford, and he taught himself to drive on a road next to the river Maas. Later, that area became part of a sea harbour for the very large cruise ships of the Holland-America line.

After our schooling, we needed to prepare for the working world. Three quarters of the class took typing lessons, but our parents thought that we needed more education. We wanted to become gymnastics teachers, but we were too short. We began

1919.The van Daelen Children: 3 Dimensional Photo figurine of Simon, Aat, Jeanne and Rie.

a pharmacy course in 1933; after the two-year course, we were apprenticed to the local pharmacy, Ooster Pharmacy in Rotterdam. It wasn't very difficult for us, and we enjoyed it very much. We went to Amsterdam to take our final exams, and then I got a job as an assistant pharmacist in a local Rotterdam pharmacy, Pharmacy Meerburg at Rusthoflaan 34 in Krooswijk. There were a number of Jewish people employed there. I liked my job at the pharmacy and had three particular friends: Hetty Monasch, Emmy de Bruyn, and Lenie Schrammeyer.

My sister couldn't find a job for a year and a half: there was so much unemployment then. She volunteered to work for a few hours every week, but she had so much time on her hands that she was bored stiff. She embroidered a very large tablecloth as a gift for me. I still have it. She could play the piano beautifully, much better than I could. Fortunately, the pharmacy eventually hired her.

My job was shiftwork. I worked mornings till 1:00, and returned for the evening shift from 5:30 to 9:00. This meant I could go swimming or play tennis every afternoon from 2:00 to 4:00. I took hair-styling lessons, too, for one year I liked learning how to make curls. The models we practiced on were given five cents for volunteering to allow the styling students to use an electric curling iron on their hair. After my hair-styling lessons, I rushed home on my bike. My mother always made something for me to eat because I had to be back at the pharmacy for my evening shift. The strange thing was that I was never tired. At the pharmacy, I often had to help with the difficult jobs, like getting dirt out of someone's eyes. I think they chose me to help because I never got in a panic. Once, a student group brought in a student with a head wound. As I was the only one there, I had to take care of him. I called the police, and they took him to the hospital.

I could live on my salary, which was eighty guilders, because I was still living at my parents' house. I had one savings account, for my salary. My colleague lived on her own and really had not much left over from paying for the essentials to spend on luxuries. I remember my first paycheque: I biked like crazy to the Bijenkorf (a store like The Bay) because I had seen a white sweater there and I bought it, and with a box full of éclairs, I biked home. I still like éclairs very much.

My father didn't like it at all that every month I had to work one nightshift a week by myself in the pharmacy and I had to sleep alone above the shop. He was quite right, but if I had refused, they would have fired me right away. I only had a problem once: in front of the window of the pharmacy there was an uproar around a drunken man with a cut to his jugular vein. I called the police right away, put the "closed" sign on the door, and turned out the lights. The police came and took the man to the hospital. The next morning, his wife brought me a box of cakes to thank me for calling the police.

Everyone in the family at that time was Orthodox, but we never kept all the Orthodox rituals and we never kept a kosher house; we never went to synagogue, and my mother never lit candles on Friday night. But we never ate shellfish, pork, or other foods that were forbidden by Jewish dietary laws. My grandfather was the Orthodox one, and he kept the Sabbath. When we were young, we didn't know anything about anti-Semitism. We didn't know at school that "who we were" really meant "what we were". Even when I heard someone yell to his friend in the street about us, shouting: "There are those Jews wearing those glasses," I didn't realized what they meant. My parents had many friends, and they were all Jewish.

In those days, people volunteered a great deal for charity. Aunt Marie's husband, Uncle Bram, had a good shoe shop, and he always had small baskets on his counter for charities such as the Jewish orphanage, the Jewish relief house for the poor, etc. Every customer put some coins in these baskets. He also put ten cents from every purchase into the baskets.

Author's Note: *Before the Second World War, a sort of social harmony resulted from the fact that many Dutch people only interacted with members of their faith: Catholics with Catholics, Protestants with Protestants, and Jews with other Jews. This is called Verzuiling, or compartmentalization. Each religion was represented in society as a silo and had its own social institutions, including newspapers, schools, and sports clubs. This turned out to be a disadvantage for the Jews when the deportations began in 1942 because they could not easily reach out to those of other religions for help. Despite being a minority, Dutch Jews were not specifically discriminated against. Anti-Semitism on a large scale was brought in by the Nazis in 1940.*

CHAPTER 2

Falling in Love

Then boys came into my life. Rinus was the first one; he was very affectionate for he was very much in love with me. He often came to the pharmacy to pick me up and was a very special kind of person. He always went to the library to study old manuscripts and old poets, like Joost van den Vondel. He had a great sense of humour but not much contact with young people his age. I didn't notice that. Like me, he was short. We went for walks and kissed a lot. Later, during the war, Rinus was whipped to death by the Nazis. He was wearing his Star of David and walking alone in the market square. This was forbidden to Jews, and they caught him and whipped him till he died.

Author's Note: *At the end of April 1942, the Dutch police issued, under Nazi orders, a decree that all Jews would have to wear a Jodenster, a palm-sized Star of David, in plain view on their clothing when in public. Not wearing the Jodenster would incur heavy punishment; even so, most Jews were averse to wearing these Stars as they felt branded. At the same time, Jews were forbidden to wear medals or other badges of honour. Because they were owned by Jews, all the textile factories had*

Clockwise from top left: Rie and Jeanne at 16 (1931); Skating on the Kralingerplas in Rotterdam (1930); Simon showed movies regularly to his friends, in the attic of their house in Rotterdam (1931); Aat in his parents' house; Aat and Simon 1931; Rie is on the right (1930).

Clockwise from top: Two of Rie's good friends from the pharmacy. Emmy de Bruin, who kept many of Rie's valuables safe during the war, is on the right;

July 14, 1937 - Knokke, Belgium. Alice Witsenhuijsen, Rie and Jeanne;

Rie and her colleagues from the pharmacy in Rotterdam. 1935. Rie is on the right.

Inside of Rie's Pharmacy book, printed in 1918. The oak leaf was dried by Rie in 1935.

been closed by that time except for one, in Enschede, where the Stars were produced from big rolls of yellow cloth. They were not given out for free, but cost four Dutch cents and a clothing ration coupon.
(National Dagblad April 10, 1942)

We belonged to a Jewish club of about 100 young people over the age of 18. There was a film one week, and dancing lessons the next week. It was always me, rather than Jeanne, who was first on the dance floor or who went out with a boy. We went skating when there was ice—natural ice, not artificial ice. We played tennis a lot.

At the Rotterdam tennis club in the summer of 1932, when I was 17, I met Elkan Katan. He was studying to be a registered accountant at the University of Rotterdam. Elkan had beautiful wavy curls, which I loved, and he didn't wear glasses. At first, he came to the tennis club a lot and we got to know each other very well, but then his studies became more serious and we hardly saw each other for two years. When he was at home, his mother, Juul, took full possession of him. Juul had a large shop, and all the brothers and sisters left the house when Elkan, her second son, came so that their mother could have him all to herself. She had been widowed for a long time. Elkan's father, Nathan, had died on May 5, 1919, when Elkan was 7 years old. Nathan was born on April 24, 1867, in Maassluis, close to Rotterdam.

Our relationship became serious at a big fundraiser to collect money for the Jewish German fugitives. Everyone went to that party in evening dress. We found each other in the Bierstube (beer cellar), and from that time on, we were a couple. My father was really pleased with Elkan, and he would play pool with him on Sunday afternoons, but my mother was very nervous and called him "sir" now and then.

When we finished our dancing lessons, our group of ten went over to the Jewish butcher, who sold nice meat sandwiches—for

Clockwise from top: Oma Juul and her five kids;

1940 - Oma Juul Katan on her 60th birthday;

1938 - Elkan;

Oma Juul's store, Magazijn Nederland;

Photos of the happy couple Rie and Elkan.

Advertisement for the store where Rie and Elkan bought their engagment rings. The handwriting on the right says, For Rie's lover!"

instance, a sandwich with half liver, half pastrami or a bun with sausage. Of course he didn't sell non-kosher food, such as bacon or ham. The butcher gave us a glass of tea for free, and the price of the cheapest sandwich was 5 cents. My sister Jeanne had no income at that time, so she always ordered the cheapest sandwich—the one with liver. Elkan always bought me a warm veal sandwich, and once he gave Jeanne one, too.

Now I feel terrible because I (who had a good salary) never even offered to buy Jeanne a sandwich. It never occurred to me, and now I feel so sorry. Never did I think to say, "Buy another kind, other than liver, and I'll pay for it." Somehow it never came into my head. Jeanne never said anything about it, and she was never jealous.

It must have been hard for Jeanne when Elkan came on Saturday nights to our house for dinner. After coffee, the three of us would go out—Jeanne would hold Elkan's arm and I would walk beside them. It was too crazy for words. When Elkan suggested we all go to the movies, she put twenty-five cents on the table, saying that she liked going with the two of us. She always paid her own way to the movies. She didn't want Elkan to pay for her. When Elkan and I went out alone somewhere, Jeanne began to play the piano; however, the moment I closed the front door, I heard her burst into tears. She was certainly lonelier than I was.

Elkan and I got engaged in 1938 when I was 22 years old. He was living at Nicolaas Beetsstraat 19, in Eindhoven, at the time, working for Philips Electronics as an accountant. His mother was not pleased about our engagement; I wasn't sure why, but I think she wanted to keep her brightest and favorite son to herself. We had a fantastic engagement party. For our engagement we saved square coins, five cents each. Everybody in the van Daelen family turned their wallets out at the end of each week and there were always square coins to be found for us. With that money, Elkan and I bought our crystal glassware. Can you imagine—twelve wine glasses, twelve port glasses, twelve champagne glasses, and twelve gin glasses? At that time, we thought we could not live without having the complete sets. During the war, they were put in hiding, and there are still many remaining. They were all made from very thin crystal. Later, I bought thicker glasses, which were easier to wash without breaking.

We saved money for everything. There were many engagement presents. I received about six sugar-and-milk sets, and I exchanged them at the store where we had bought everything. In 1938, I bought the cups from there. They were porcelain with gold feet, very fine. We saved for the large service, and bought it for sixty guilders: twelve plates, twelve soup plates, twelve breakfast plates, four serving dishes, eight dill plates, and much more. I was happy that they were all hidden by friends during the war, and they are still in my cupboard today. They are not valuable, but they are good porcelain, white with a golden and blue rim.

PART 2

Speech delivered by Seyss-Inquart in Amsterdam's Concert Gebouw, winter 1941

"The Jews, for us, are not Dutch. They are those enemies with whom we can come to neither an armistice nor to peace . . . We will beat the Jews wherever we meet them, and those who join them must bear the consequences. The Führer has declared that the Jews have played their final act in Europe, and therefore they have played their final act."

CHAPTER 3

Germany Invades the Neutral Country of the Netherlands

Author's Note: *On May 10, 1940, at 4 a.m., Waalhaven military airport in the harbour area south of Rotterdam was bombed by the Germans and then occupied. This was the beginning of the war for the Dutch people. At the same time as the bombing of the Waalhaven, German troops crossed the border. They marched North to Rotterdam and The Hague, and heavy fighting raged in the Rotterdam harbour. The bridges at Moerdijk and Gennep, on the Dutch-German border, were taken undamaged.*

Two days later, the Dutch air force had practically been wiped out, with the R.A.F. otherwise engaged in France and Belgium.

Four days later, on May 14, the town centre was firebombed; it was a windy day, so the flames spread very quickly, and all of beautiful downtown Rotterdam was destroyed. This forced the Netherland government to surrender.

The night of the invasion, the Germans decreed that in order to avoid providing targets for bombings, all citizens must cover their windows with dark curtains or pieces of black paper. No lights were allowed after dark: This included streetlights, ferry lights, and bicycle lights-all public as well as private light sources. This made it very dangerous for workers returning home after nightfall. Several people drowned in the canals as a direct result of these blackouts (verduistering). Each day, the front page of every newspaper would tell people when that night's blackout would begin.

We knew that Queen Wilhelmina had an agreement with Hitler that the Germans would not attack Holland: He broke that agreement. When the Germans began to bomb the military airport and harbour in Waalhaven, South of Rotterdam on 10 May 1940, my brothers and my sister heard a lot of noise at 6:00 in the morning. We took our bikes and went to the Maas River, and we saw the planes coming, dropping all the parachuted soldiers into the water. There were so many. There were tanks coming over the bridge, and there were Germans everywhere. We realized that we had better go home quickly. The town was surrounded by Germans and we had to make a wide detour to get to our home in the west of Rotterdam, fairly near the Zoo. We shouted to everyone, "The war is coming. The war is coming."

It was my brother's birthday, and a very hot day. My father said that-war or not-he was staying in his bed; he was not going outside. My mother was so nervous—she must have gone twenty times to look out the window. My elder brother, Simon, was very quiet and murmured, "We'll see what comes of this." Elkan and I were not yet married, and he was working in Eindhoven, but he managed to come back to Rotterdam to be with me.

Our house was fairly close to the central station and we could see the trains coming and going. Rotterdam was firebombed on May 14 and burned for three days. There were two synagogues in Rotterdam, and both were bombed at that time. We heard the marching and the music and the shouting in the streets. That was to frighten the people. But this was not the worst for the Jews: That came later.

Although it was a luxury, we had two cars in the family— my father and my brother, Simon, each had a car. The first thing that happened was that Simon's car was stolen. It was a new car, a Chevrolet costing 2000 guilders. He was very upset that his new car was stolen, but we reminded him that at least we were all still alive.

Author's Note: *On the morning of May 13, 1940, three days after the German invasion, Queen Wilhelmina left on a British destroyer from Hoek van Holland and travelled to Harwich in England. That same night, she was welcomed to the Liverpool Street Station in London by King George VI. One day later, she was followed by her cabinet.*

Queen Wilhelmina and her cabinet, despite being in exile, continued to govern the Netherlands as well as they could from London. The Minister of Justice, Professor Gerbrandy, was aware of the importance of the BBC, and he and Wilhelmina established a radio station called Radio Orange (Oranje), or The Voice of the Fighting Netherlands. The station would broadcast for 15 minutes at the same time each day. Wilhelmina used Radio Orange to broadcast 34 speeches; this was the only way she could communicate with her people, who were avid listeners. Among other topics, she used these broadcasts to forcefully condemn the deportation of her Jewish compatriots. Although radios were forbidden in Holland, many did listen secretly to the broadcasts. Lou de Jong, a Jew who later became a major historian of the Holocaust, worked for Radio Orange for the whole of its five-year operating period.
(Wilhelmina, by Elsevier)

Our Queen Wilhelmina and the government fled to London, England. Elkan and I tried to leave the country too. We went to the Hook of Holland to try to find a boat. Elkan and I found a skipper who charged us 1000 guilders in advance to take the two of us in his boat to England, on the condition that it was safe to go. Elkan paid him the money, and we agreed on a certain date and place. We each packed a suitcase and arrived at the agreed time and spot. But luck was certainly not with us that day: The skipper did not show up. I thought that maybe it was not safe enough for him that day, so we decided to come back the next day at the same time. We waited for three days, but the skipper never showed up—we never knew why. Perhaps he took our money and left the country. We were helpless to do anything about it. After this, it proved to be almost impossible to leave the Netherlands.

One of my uncles also tried to get away by boat. He went to the bank and withdrew 10,000 guilders, which was a fortune in those days, to pay a herring boat skipper to take him and his family early in the morning to England. He had to pay in advance, and no boat was there in the morning. They, too, were powerless to do anything about it. He and all his family died in Auschwitz.

In October, 1940, five months after the Germans occupied the Netherlands, we were married. We had waited for two years, and we didn't know what the war would bring. I had wanted a white dress for my wedding. But all the houses were destroyed in Rotterdam

and everything was in chaos. All the surrounding area of City Hall, where the civil ceremony was held, was destroyed. So I thought that I couldn't insist on a white wedding dress and there was no white fabric available anyway. Instead, I wore a royal blue dress with white gloves and white veil for my wedding, and I carried a bouquet of white carnations. There was one car for us, and we rented a tramcar for

31 October 1941 - Wedding Rie and Elkan in Rotterdam. Her wedding dress was blue because there was no white fabric available. All the shops had been bombarded.

1940, October 31. Wedding of Rie and Elkan. All the van Daelens in this photo were gassed, except Rie.

all our family and friends. That was the only way to get to City Hall. The religious ceremony was held in a secret synagogue that was entered through a garage; all the other synagogues in Rotterdam had been bombed. The rabbi who married us sang so beautifully. I have heard that later, in Auschwitz, he also sang beautifully.

In the secret Garage Synagogue.

Wedding photo of Aat and Adele - 1940.

Wedding photo of Simon and Alice - 1940.

My brothers rented a party hall, the only one which had not been bombed, and at one o'clock in the afternoon everyone was waiting outside. We had to wait because the Germans were watching a boxing match in the hall, and all the soldiers had to leave before the Jews were allowed to enter.

My family sent all the photo albums to me that they had. You can't believe how many photo albums they have sent. My father sent his tallit (prayer shawl) to me, too. For our honeymoon, we took the tramway from Rotterdam to Amsterdam and back.

Elkan had lived in Eindhoven in the southeastern part of Holland for the preceding couple of years and had worked for Philips. But now he got a very good job in The Hague as a chartered accountant for the Advisory Office for Organization and Efficiency. Mr. van de Bunt was the main partner in the company. He was to prove to be a wonderful friend, and a true help to us in the dark days ahead. He and his wife, with initiative and courage, saved our lives, at a time when many others were turning against Jewish people and collaborating with the Nazis. The company had two offices, one in Amsterdam and one in The Hague: The Amsterdam office was on Dam square, on the street called het Rokin, above the Industrial Club; in The Hague, the office was called "de Kantoor Machine Gids" and it was on Kneuterdijk. Elkan worked in both offices.

We moved to Amsterdam right after our marriage. Believe me, I could have cried. We had such a good circle of Jewish friends in Eindhoven that I was always happy to visit. But I had never been in Amsterdam, and we found it very difficult to find a nice flat. When we moved there, Elkan's work was not in Amsterdam, but in The Hague. Can you imagine, when you first get married, you have a perfectly clean new house, and your husband leaves on the train early in the morning and arrives home around 7 in the evening. He was tired, so we went to bed early. I had nothing to do, so I suggested that I find some work—something to do. "No," Elkan said, "I earn the money. You can't work." I slept every afternoon because I didn't have anything to do, and I didn't have any friends in Amsterdam.

Our Amsterdam apartment was at de Lekstraat 33. It was at the corner, and next to us were a park and a new synagogue. We never went to the synagogue, but it was there. The apartment was very nice and modern, and we decorated it very well. It had a large living room; connected to it was a nice bedroom; next to it was a parlour, like a sitting room; and there was also a guest room with a Murphy double bed. This room soon also held a little blue baby bed, which I have kept all these years for the first grandchild. If some of the children don't want it, I don't care. I'll keep it for the second grandchild, and I hope that I will live long enough to enjoy that.

We had no telephone—the Germans had forbidden it by then—but Mr. van Oudkerk, the Jewish butcher on the corner, had a telephone. I sometimes asked him if I could use his telephone to call my mother in Rotterdam. It was expensive at that time (sixty cents for three minutes), but I called her several times per week. She was very lonely because all her children had moved away from home. She was very happy to hear from me. In the fall of 1940, three of my mother's children had married within two months of one another: Aat, my younger brother, got married at the beginning of September; Simon, my older brother, married at the end of September; and Elkan and I married on the 31st of October. So, all three left home at the same time.

But now, the legislation against the Jews began. Jews were not allowed to have a non-Jewish maid. My mother's maid had worked for the family for 17 years, but she had to leave. She cried and said that she had been there so long—why did she have to leave? There was misery all over. Also, we were not allowed to play tennis anymore in non-Jewish clubs. This happened so suddenly: One day, I had arranged to meet a friend at my tennis club, and when I arrived for our tennis match, there was a sign on the gate: "Forbidden for Jews." I was devastated. We Jews were no longer allowed to go out into the street anymore after 8:00 p.m., or shop in the regular shops. We couldn't buy anything anymore. We had to go to the Jewish market in the Lekstraat only at a certain time—between 2:00 and 4:00. At that market we were allowed to shop and buy anything we wanted twice a week. We didn't feel very comfortable there because at the entrance of the market there was a member of the NSB (National Socialist Movement) or a German, and later on, as the Nazis tightened their anti-Jewish program, there were Dutch policemen. But that was the only place we could buy food.

Author's Note: *Within a week of the surrender, Hitler appointed Reich Commissioner Arthur Seyss-Inquart to rule occupied Holland. He was an open anti-Semite, and moved into the Clingendael mansion in The Hague. This* *is traditionally where the Dutch prime minister lives. The German SS played a dominant role in implementing anti-Jewish measures under Seyss-Inquart. Late in 1940, he decreed that all Jewish-owned businesses must be registered (including the Brothers van Daelen Oil and Grease Factory). In early 1941, the requirement for registration was extended to the Jews themselves. If they refused, they would be punished by heavy fines and/or five years in prison. In accordance with the Dutch predilection to obey the law no matter what, almost every Jew went along with the registration. They were required to carry identity cards with the letter J printed on them, without which they could not obtain food ration coupons. By the end of 1941, Jews were no longer permitted at non-Jewish clubs.*

Mr. van Oudkerk had a big butcher shop, and in the basement he had put a table tennis table. In the evenings after 8:00 we went to his basement and met some new friends—five families—and played table tennis. That gave us some coziness and fun. We were all from the same neighbourhood. The butcher made his own sausages and treated us now and then with a delicious piece of special sausage. But after a while, he told us that he could not offer us those treats anymore because he could not afford it. But he had sweetbreads (zwezerik) that we could fry to extract the fat. Actually, we enjoyed that tremendously. We used it for a long time for frying and everything tasted delicious with that fat. It was also used on our sandwiches because there was nothing else.

The van Daelen factory was the first to introduce antifreeze for cars; they made it themselves. The Germans were very anxious to get their hands on the secret for its production. My brother, Simon, was summoned to a German office to tell them how antifreeze was made. It wasn't such a big secret; if you knew a bit of chemistry, it's very easy. But at that time it was a secret. The Germans offered to make him an honourary Nazi. Simon was the one who went to the synagogue, so he refused. So they threatened to send him to a work camp like the others, however he did not give in.

Later, on the 1st of November 1942, the van Daelen factory plus two of our private houses were handed over to the Nazis. Hendrik van Daelen had to hand in a statement of all his properties and debts to the Bank Lippmann & Rosenthal. All his property (the factory plus his house and contents) was valued at only NLF 213,056.65, which was the Dutch currency at the time. This was far too low! His debts were in the form of two smaller mortgages amounting to NLF 69,150; the balance was NLF 143,906.65. To run the company, a German president, a Verwalter, was installed, and everyone was fired, including my father and my grandfather, who were the owners. Suddenly, they had no income. Fortunately, my family still had some money, so they could cope.

Elkan, too, was dismissed from Mr. van de Bunt's company after the 1941 edict that forbade Jews to be employed by Gentiles. He was asked to join the Jewish Council and work for them as the main bookkeeper for the vegetable market. I still have the booklet that Mr. van de Bunt's company published to commemorate its tenth anniversary. It was published on June 16, 1943, and included a photograph and the signature of each of the ten employees: Elkan's photograph and name are there. The booklet included a caricature of each employee. The sketch of Elkan shows him standing in the doorway of a fruit and vegetable store; a sign next to the doorway reads: "The little boss"—obviously a comment on his diminutive height and strong personality. It was so good of them to include Elkan in this anniversary booklet, as so many companies were distancing themselves from everything to do with the Jews. The sketch even made reference to his position on the Jewish Council.

Author's Note: *The Jewish Council, set up by the Germans in Amsterdam, was a group of prominent Jews who were forced to work as administrators under strict orders from the Germans. They were responsible for obtaining labour for the Germans, allocating housing assignments to the Jews, collecting taxes, helping the old and sick, and meeting deportation quotas. In*

*exchange, they attempted to negotiate better living conditions
for people in the Amsterdam ghetto.*

Shortly after our move to Amsterdam, Elkan was ordered by
the Nazis to go to a work camp in Holland to work in the fields.
This was a camp set up by the Dutch government for the German
Jews who had fled from Germany. Much later, I realized that this

1943. Jewish Council (Joodse Raad) in Amsterdam. Elkan, 2nd row from top on the right. was
the only surviver of this group.

Jewish Council, Amsterdam, July 1943

was Camp Westerbork. I suggested to Elkan that we have a baby because I was afraid that if he was sent away, I would have nothing of him left. Everyone told me I was crazy and wondered what I would do with a baby in these terrible times. Elkan did not dismiss the idea at all; in fact, he agreed. We were looking forward to having a baby. Pregnancy would delay our being rounded up for the work camp, so we were a little bit protected.

We all had identity cards which had a big "J" on them, which identified us as Jews. To escape from being rounded up by the Germans, we knew we would need papers with Gentile names and no big "J" on them. Elkan knew how to get false identity papers. He had a business connection with the non-Jewish owner of a dairy plant in Amsterdam, who worked in the underground resistance

1942 - Identiy Card for Elkan (accountant) with J (Jew).

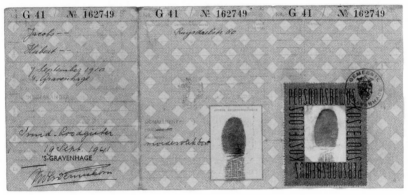

1941 - False Idenitiy Card with Elkan's new name "Hubert Jacobs (plumber)"

movement and was willing to provide us with false identity papers. We knew that these people in the resistance movement were risking their lives to help us Jews, and we were so grateful.

He got those papers for us. He gave us back some hope of escaping the round-up of Jews that had begun. But Elkan had a lot of relatives and we ended up giving our false identity papers to some of them who needed them to travel on the trains to their hiding place. I thought that we would be all right because we had a Sperrstempel. A select few had this exemption stamp including the members of the Jewish council. The stamp was placed upon Jewish identity papers, which delayed the deportation date of that person. Like everyone else, we hoped that the war would be over before our deportation date arrived. Later, one may think about

1941 - Rie's Identity Card.

this differently, but we were not such bad people that we could refuse to help others. We were already indebted to Elkan's business colleague, who had been so willing to help us.

Author's Note: *In January 1942, at the Wannsee Conference near Berlin, a group of senior officials of the German regime approved the adoption of the "Final Solution to the Jewish Question." This meant the deportation of the Jews of Europe and North Africa to labour camps and ultimate extermination in occupied Eastern Europe. Different methods of extermination were discussed, and racial categories were established for identifying Jews. Minutes of the Wannsee Conference were not found until 1947.*

Deportation Schedules July 1942—September 1943:
1942

- **June:** *The Jewish Council was informed that Jews would have to go to Germany to work under the supervision of the police. However, because relatively few Jews reported to the* **Zentralstelle**, *the central agency, by July 14, the German police arrested approximately 750 Jews in mass raids. This strategy worked well, and over 6,000 Jews reported for the "labour draft," and were shipped to Camp Westerbork between July 15 and July 31.*

- **August:** *In the extra issue of* **Het Joodsche Weekblad**, *The Jewish Weekly, published that month, the German police let it be known that non-reporters for the "labor draft" would be arrested and sent to Mauthausen. In addition, they conducted two mass raids in Amsterdam and rounded up thousands of Jews. However, it appears that the officials of the Jewish Council stationed at the assembly point succeeded in helping many to escape.*

- **September:** *Large nightly raids began in Amsterdam, resulting in the capture of 300-500 Jews per night.*

- **October:** *The rounding up of Jews in the other big cities, especially Rotterdam, began. The work camp, located in the east of Holland and housing between 7,000 and 8,000 Jews, were closed.*

- **November:** *Those Jews who were granted exemptions because they were employed in factories working for the German armed forces were arrested at their places of work, and along with their families, sent to Camp Westerbork.*

1943

- **January:** *Institutionalized persons, such as Jewish orphans, the aged, and the sick, were rounded up. Exemptions for German Jewish veterans of WWI were cancelled.*

- **March:** *Jews living outside of Amsterdam had to report for deportation, and raids were conducted in the provinces. Deportations to Sobibor began.*

- **May:** *All remaining Jews living in Amsterdam, except those with exemptions, were ordered to report. Since only one quarter arrived, the Germans ordered the Jewish Council* to designate 7,000 of its own employees for deportation. Because so few reported, the Germans rounded up 3,000 Jews from the centre of Amsterdam on May 26.

- **June:** 5,700 Jews were captured in a mass raid in Amsterdam.
- **September 29:** 3,000 Jews, including the leaders of the Jewish Council, were arrested in Amsterdam, and 7,000 Jews from the provinces were rounded up in simultaneous raids. The final step was the last big razzia in Amsterdam and the liquidation of the Jewish Council.

(Werner Warmbrunn: The Dutch Under German Occupation, 1940-1945)

1940 - Jeanne outside her parents' residence, at Simon and Alice van Daelen's wedding.

CHAPTER 4

Jeanne is the First to Go

My sister, Jeanne, was the first to go to the camps. Jeanne got notice that she was not allowed to work in the pharmacy in Rotterdam anymore. She was dismissed because she was a Jew, and her employer, Mr. Meerburg, was pro-Nazi. Now she had no money to live on, so she moved back home, which my mother loved.

In Amsterdam, there was only one Jewish pharmacy. I went there and asked if my sister from Rotterdam could work there: She was fully qualified. They were glad that she could come, as they had too much work for their current staff. There were a lot of Jews in south Amsterdam, and this was the only pharmacy they could shop at. So I asked Elkan and he agreed that it would be excellent for her to come and stay with us. This was devastating to my mother because now all her children had left home.

Jeanne had to have a permit from the Germans to work in the pharmacy. On July 16th, 1942, Jeanne went to the centre of Amsterdam where there was a Jewish office that administered the permits. That very day, the Nazis, in green uniforms, came in there and took all the Jews away. My sister was sitting next to a typist answering the employment questions. The typist told her to stay quiet and maybe the Nazis wouldn't notice her. It worked: They left without rounding her up.

However, when she left the office and went out into the hall, one of the green-uniformed Nazis saw her and said, "You, too." So unfortunately, she was caught. About 50 people had been in the office, and they were told to return to their homes and report back the next night at midnight with one suitcase. They were given a list of things to pack: These items had to be packed in two parts, one for the trip and one for their next destination. They were not allowed to bring any live animals. They were going to be sent to a work camp in the east. Here is Jeanne's list: 1 suitcase, 1 pair of work boots, 2 pairs of socks, 2 pairs of underwear, 2 undershirts, 1 work suit, 2 woolen blankets, 2 sets of bed linen (sheets), 1 bowl for soup, 1 mug, 1 spoon, 1 pullover sweater, 1 towel, toiletries, food for a three-day march, and valid ration coupons.

Author's Note: *On May 1, 1941, Jewish doctors, pharmacists, and translators for non-Jews were told they would no longer be employed. On June 26, 1942, the Jewish Council was informed that men and women between the ages of 16 and 40 would have to be registered for 'police-controlled labor contingents' to work in Germany. Starting on July 12, the Dutch police came personally to round people up; the active involvement of the Germans was limited. In the month of July, a total of eight transport trains left Amsterdam for the detention camp Westerbork, setting the pattern for the next 15 months. On July 15, the Germans began the deportation of Dutch Jews from Westerbork to concentration camps in Germany and Poland. By September of 1944, about 100 trains had carried more than 100,000 people to Auschwitz, Sobibor, Theresienstadt and Bergen-Belsen.*

The family had a day-and-a-half to do something. My father had a lot of connections, and there were options open to us. We could get her false papers and send her to Belgium, where she could go into hiding. She insisted that she was going to go because I was pregnant. She said, "I don't want that because if I don't report myself, the Germans will come and it will be you who is picked up and you are pregnant. You and Elkan are starting a family, so I have to report. I'm not going into hiding because that is the wrong thing to do, and I could never forgive myself. If I don't show up, then they will take all of you instead. Don't worry. I am a strong woman. I will survive."

She was such a hero—she said that she would save herself somehow. She said it was her duty not to endanger me. What could we say? I think I would have done the same. She was like me—we were always trying to fix things.

So my father and mother in Rotterdam asked for a travel permit to accompany her back to Amsterdam to say goodbye. They stayed in our apartment that night. Father and Mother slept with Jeanne in the one bedroom, and Elkan and I were in the other bedroom. I cannot tell you how much hurt and sorrow there was. We talked the entire night about everything.

Jeanne asked me if she could have this and that. We dressed her in every dress that she could wear. She was as slim as could be, but we piled the dresses on her until she looked like the Michelin man. She complained laughingly that she could hardly walk, but we said that she should take everything that she could with her. And so on July 17, 1942, she left our apartment, reporting at midnight to the tram place. The next morning, my parents went back to Rotterdam. It was very difficult to watch my parents walk away from our apartment—two old people, about 55 years old—walking away, to probably never see their child again.

Jeanne was put on the train to Camp Westerbork— the camp in the northeast of Holland. In the train, Jeanne wrote a farewell letter and threw it out of the window.

There were always Dutch people searching along the train tracks, and so my family got a last letter from her:

Dear S. [Simon] A. [Aat], L.[Alice], Dé [Adele],
Amsterdam 17 July 1942

This is then a farewell letter. I am a victim of a 'razzia'
[rounding up] of the Grüne [Nazi police]. I was forced to
give my signature 'voluntarily' so that I would not be sent
to a concentration camp in Germany, but instead to a labor
camp in Germany. And all efforts have been in vain to get my
signature deleted.

When a 'mof' [German] once has his prey, he will not let
go. Try to stay out of the hands of those guys! I am now a
victim and go there in full realization that I will never return.

Be comforting to Pa and Ma and do not worry too much. I
will try to get through this. Each bomb that falls on Germany
will not fall on my head. It is war and I must take the
consequences of being a victim. I have lost the war, but you all
have to try to win it.

Give all my friends my greetings as it is impossible to write
to all for lack of time. We have done all we could to get free, so
it is not our fault. For me, this had to be.

I am going in full trust, tell that to A.B.V. and will always
keep faith despite what I will experience!
Saturday night at 01.30 the train will leave.

Stay strong, always continue to fight and support each
other. G'd bless you all, further keep good spirits.
But lost is already lost and that should not be.

Love,

Jeanne van Daelen

Jeanne was kept in Camp Westerbork until the end of
September. We never heard from her when she was in the camp,
and we didn't know what it would be like for her in that camp.
Later on, we received a letter from someone else about Westerbork,
which told us a little bit about the camp. It was a wet place—all

mud and wet. People's feet just sank in the mud. Even though she wore all her clothes at once, she was still cold. We also heard that there wasn't food enough for everyone.

> **Author's Note:** *Camp Westerbork was built in 1938 in the northeast of Holland near Assen in Drenthe to house both legal and illegal German Jewish refugees. At that time, the Dutch government had decided that all refugees would be accommodated in camps rather than live freely in the community. On the first day of the invasion, it was taken over by the Germans. On July 15, 1942, the first train left Westerbork for Auschwitz, with almost 4,000 Jews deported in the next two weeks. Westerbork was to become the final collection point for all Jews in Holland before their deportation to the Eastern death camps. The last train left September 5, 1944; Anne Frank was among the 1,019 Jews deported on that last transport to Auschwitz.*

Life at Camp Westerbork: Westerbork ran the best-equipped hospital in Eastern Holland, with 1,800 beds, a staff of more than a 1,000, and 120 doctors in 1943. As well, Westerbork contained a children's school, a nursery, an orphanage, a synagogue, a small mortuary, a jail, a shoe-repair factory, and workshops for tailoring and bookbinding. Everyone worked as slave labour—in administration, in the shops disassembling wrecked aircraft or recovering batteries, or on the farm, which provided most of the food for the camp. Although conditions in the camp were bad, everyone was terrified of being put on the weekly train to the East. The BBC regularly reported on the topic of mass murder by gassing in Poland, but it is believed that the Jews in Westerbork refused to accept the idea. They were afraid of the trains but rejected the idea of death camps. (Jacob Boas: The Story of Transit Camp Westerbork)

Anne Frank's diary contains this October 9th, 1942, passage: *"We think that most people will be murdered. The English radio speaks of gassing, and maybe that is the quickest method of killing. I'm totally upset."*

At first, we heard that Jeanne had been sent to Auschwitz and put to work for a while until she died of dysentery. But later, after the war, we bought and read the official record of the Dutch Jews that was published in the book called "In Memoriam".

Jeanne was gassed on the very day she arrived in Auschwitz, 24 Sept 1942, at the age of 27. We didn't know. In Holland, no one knew about Auschwitz during the war.

Jeanne van Daelen, 1915 - 1942

CHAPTER 5

My Family is Rounded Up

After Jeanne was gone, I went to Rotterdam alone and had a talk with my brothers. I told Elkan that I must warn the family about the round-ups for the work camps in the east. In Amsterdam there was the Jewish Council—a group of elite people selected by the Germans—a professor of this, a doctor of that. My husband was linked with the Council too, after 1940. They had to inform the Jews of all the anti-Jewish legislation, and in some cases, to assist in its implementation. Because of information from the Jewish Council, I knew that things were very bad for the Jews. I wanted my family to say that they were ill and couldn't do work duty in the camps in the east. But, in fact, everyone in my family was healthy, and they didn't believe my warnings about the round-ups. But we in Amsterdam knew so much more than people in Rotterdam about what was actually happening because Rotterdam had no Jewish Council.

And so it happened again. My mother phoned and told me that my younger brother, Aat, had to go to the police station. He was told it was just a little administrative detail. He thought it was about his driver's license. He went, not knowing that he would never return. After three hours the police came and picked up his wife, Adèle de Vries. Adele's mother lived three quarters of an hour from her only daughter and was a bad walker. She hurried to my mother's house hoping for some comfort, but what comfort could there be? Aat and Adèle had a completely new house, as they were just married. My brothers lived on the same street—one on one side and one on the other. We had always been close together— every evening until Elkan and I moved to Amsterdam, all four of us girls got together, playing chess, etc. We had done all kinds of things together.

Aat and Adèle were sent to Camp Westerbork on October 9, 1942. Aat was able to arrange a Sperre, an exemption stamp, and their deportation was stopped. They remained in Westerbork, and Aat acted as financial controller for the Verwalter (manager). But inevitably, Aat and Adele were shipped to Auschwitz where Aat was gassed on October 28, 1943, a week after his wife, Adele, who was gassed on October 19, 1943.

My elder brother, Simon, was tall, and we always thought he was the stronger personality. But no. It developed that my younger brother, Aat, was the strong one. Simon had no money and nothing to do because the Germans had thrown my father and both my brothers out of their business. For a while, Simon filled the hours gluing a yellow Star of David on a piece of plywood which he sawed into the same shape: He hated the Star. Simon saw from his apartment a van parked outside his brother's house. He watched as all of Aat's furniture was thrown out of his window into the van. Simon collapsed.

Simon's wife, Alice Witsenhuijsen, worked for Dr. Cohen in the Rotterdam subsidiary of the Amsterdam Jewish Council. Alice had a Jewish Council card with the number A 1210 and they had a Sperre. But after Aat and Adèle were rounded up, Simon and Alice lost all initiative, and were just waiting to be picked up. But Elkan and I—we were not like that. We had another kind of outlook.

The Germans came to the Jewish retirement home where my grandparents were living. They dragged them from the retirement home, and with whips, forced them to go into the cattle wagons of the train. My grandfather, Simon van Daelen, was 81 years old, and my grandmother, Adriana Doodewaard-Cohen, was 80 years old. They were shipped immediately to Auschwitz, where he was gassed on November 2, 1942, two weeks after she was gassed on October 15, 1942. I was never able to tell my children about how cruel the Germans had been to my beloved grandparents at the train station.

Spring, 1941 - Opa Simon van Daelen's 80th birthday. L to R (back): Hendrik van Daelen, Alice, Simon, Adele, Aat and Elkan. Front: Jeanne, Sara and Rie Van Daelen.

Jochebed Katan

Author's Note: *In spite of severe reprisals, Dutch groups protested against the German treatment of the Jews. In response to the first deportations of Jews in February 1941, over 200,000 Dutch citizens participated in a general strike, the only such strike in Europe in reaction to those deportations. Germans brutally repressed the strike, which is still remembered to this day on February the 25th. Over the course of the war, several attempts were made by the resistance movement to destroy the Jewish registries to impede the Nazis' deportation plans.*

Rie's Star of David.

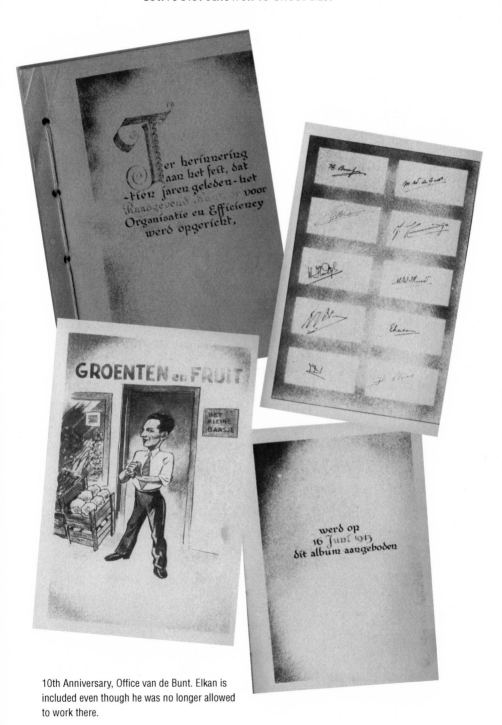

10th Anniversary, Office van de Bunt. Elkan is included even though he was no longer allowed to work there.

C H A P T E R 6

Our Baby Is Born

Elkan and I were really lucky. I have had luck my entire life—really, really. There were actually a lot of raids in the area of Amsterdam where we lived. All the Jews were picked up: We saw it. We saw the old man who lived on the first floor around the corner. He was 70 years old and he was dragged out of his bed in his pyjamas and shoved out into the street. He had to go into a truck where everyone was sitting on wooden benches. We were absolutely amazed that they did not check on us. The Registry General office was on the Plantage Middellaan, and we asked the man there why we were not picked up. He said, "Ah, you have all the luck in the world."

Our apartment overlooked a little square and there were only two houses on our little street, the Lekstraat—ours and the butcher's on the corner. The two houses were a bit apart from the others, and we think the police forgot about them. So we had a lot of luck.

The man at the Registry office told us that they did not take us because we were not registered anymore. He told us we had better re-register in order to live there. Otherwise they would plunder (puls) our house. If you were not registered, they picked you up.

Right after that, big, rough guys would come by and throw all the furniture, all your belongings, out the window into big trucks. Nobody cared if it was broken or not. Everything went into boats to Germany. That was called pulsing. These men were basically movers, who worked for the Abraham Puls Company. They were rough, ugly, and mean, and everyone called them pulsers. But we didn't re-register.

Author's Note: *The Abraham Puls Company was a Dutch removal and storage firm that was responsible for emptying the houses and apartments of Jews who had been arrested. The Jews would have about 10 minutes to gather personal belongings, and anything they did not take became the property of the Third Reich and was taken by the pulsers. Roughly 29,000 Jewish dwellings were gepulst, after which they were locked and sealed with wax. The most desirable places were then taken over as residences by Germans or Dutch Nazis.*

Jochebed, our baby, was born on Tuesday, January 12, 1943. It was a hard delivery. Dr. Van der Poort was a Jewish doctor and a friend, who came despite the regulations that forbade Jews to walk in the streets after dark. He stayed in the house, sleeping next to me in the bed for two nights because the contractions started the

Birth announcement in the Jewish newspaper.

previous Thursday. They were very heavy and then disappeared. I was given injections to get some sleep and my baby girl was born on the kitchen table. We were extremely happy when she was born, and we put an announcement in the Jewish newspaper, Het Joodsche Weekblad.

Author's Note: *Het Joodsche Weekblad, The Jewish Weekly, was the only Jewish newspaper at that time. It was published by* *the Jewish Council beginning in April 1941, when the Germans stopped all other Jewish publications. It was published every week until September 1943 and was used by the Council to publicize its activities as well as provide official statements, obituaries, and birth and wedding announcements. It was also used by the German police to communicate their regulations and threats to the Jewish population without drawing the attention of non-Jewish Dutch people.*

According to Dutch law, within five days of the birth of a child, the father had to go to the municipality to register the newborn. Elkan went to the municipality to register our baby in order to get ration coupons for her. The purchase of all food and clothing was regulated by ration coupons. He went with the collar of his winter coat pulled up and his hat on, because he was very afraid to register a Jewish baby. We had named her Jochebed, after her great-grandmother. In the Hebrew Bible, Jochebed was the mother of Aaron, Miriam, and Moses. We chose this Jewish name deliberately as a protest against the Nazi regime. Although her official name was Jochebed, we actually never called her that. Instead we began to use the name, Jeanne, after my sister. She had been rounded up when I was pregnant, and I didn't think I would ever see her again. In Dutch, the diminutive of Jeanne is Jeantje, which means "Little Jeanne."

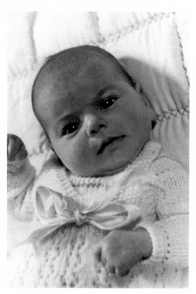

Little Jeanne, 1 month old.

Imagine, in the winter of 1943, how risky it was for Elkan to register our baby. Behind the desk was a young blond Dutch man. He just asked my husband some simple questions, and Elkan never looked him in the eye. You just never knew the politics of the man behind the desk. Our survival depended upon many people: This young man was the first to save our lives.

When all was recorded and Elkan turned to leave, the young man made a point of reassuring him by saying, "I wish her a good life. She has a beautiful Christian name, sir." He registered the baby as Christian. This man saved our baby's life. Her name was so Jewish: Jochebed was the mother of Moses, and a fine Hebrew name, and Katan was a recognized Jewish name too, meaning "small." So you see, there were also very good Dutch people – people who put their lives at risk to help the Jews.

I had hoped that my parents could come to Amsterdam for my baby's birth. However, as of September 16, 1941, travel was not permitted to Jews without a special written permit. As soon as she heard about the birth, my mother wrote me a letter.

13 January, 1943
Dearest happy parents,
My compliments on the weight of the new Jeanne. It gave us such a good feeling that you named your child after our Jeanne. She is also named after Oma van Daelen, who was a noble and sweet human being, as you might remember, and I hope that she [the baby] will follow in her footsteps in every respect and will grow up as sweet. You, Rie, are named after my sister and your daughter is named, again, after your sister. In former times, we said "Rie and Jeanne" in almost one word, and now it becomes "Rie's Jeantje" (little Jeanne). It is a new highlight, such a sweet girl, after so much sorrow lately.
You had a hard delivery, but now she is here, sweet and good, and soon you will see how you will forget the delivery and concentrate fully on the baby. We were almost able to be with you at the time of the delivery, but it did not work out.
Friday, courier Snelle Visser will bring you, from Verbiest, a chicken that you may receive by Saturday morning already. It is for a quick recovery to get your strength back: make a little

soup from it; cook the chicken thoroughly so that there is more strength in the soup than in the meat. I got a fresh chicken from Verbiest, the only place I could, because I think that with giving birth to such a heavy daughter you need a bowl of very strong chicken soup.

Thursday morning at 10 o'clock we received the letter from Elkan and in the afternoon at 3 o'clock the birth announcement card. The last one I love very much and it was finished beautifully. I will keep it with the other souvenirs from all of you. The biggest part is still to come for me, when I see little Jeanne. That name sounds so familiar...

Pa will bring a pair of socks for the baby when he comes. I believe that they will fit and if they do I will knit another pair, tell Pa when he comes. I was already in the street at 8 o'clock this morning, it was pitch dark and it rained heavily, to post this first letter because it will take another day before you receive it.

Now, dear children, all the best to the new mother, Jeantje, and not to forget, Elkan.
Much love from
Pa and your Mother

Though my parents could not come to Amsterdam for my baby's birth, my father came to visit us later, however my mother was not allowed to come with him. Simon and Alice sent a gift, which Simon had made himself—a birth plate made from cheesecloth and plaster. He had shaped the dish on the cover of a cheese plate. He sent this letter with the birth plate:

27 January, 1943
Beloved little niece,
Although I do not know you yet, as you have just become part of the family, I am writing you this letter as soon as possible. You have already given me lots of trouble! How can this be? Before you were born, I planned to have a birth-tile made for

you. But this plan could not be executed, as there is such a shortage of raw materials.

That's why I decided to make it myself and here is the result.

Ask your Daddy if he has a small nail to hang it on the wall. It has to be hung facing East as 'Mizrach'. He will know what that means.

And, little Jeanne, here are 3 oranges, which Auntie Alice bought for you with our ration coupons.

I hope soon to visit you and talk to you in person,

With greetings to all,
Simon.

I treasured both those letters, and have them still. Soon after this letter, their *Sperre* ran out, and Simon and Alice were rounded up and shipped to Sobibor where they were gassed on April 30, 1943.

My best friend from Rotterdam, Lenie Schrammeyer, came to visit, too. She had worked at the pharmacy with me. We gave Lenie a lot of our valuables, such as silverware, jewelry, and photo albums to take back with her to Rotterdam. She was not Jewish, and we believed they would be safer with her. She was a wonderful friend, and after the war, she gave them all back to us.

Some people can be trusted and others cannot. We gave Mr. Caron some of our belongings, and we expected him to give them back to us after the war. However, to our dismay, he would not. He told us at that time that my father had said that all of it was a gift to him. I was furious, and Elkan got quite angry and started to argue with him. In the meantime I peeked into the bedroom and as soon as I saw the two hand-knotted bed rugs next to the bed, I began to roll one up. Those rugs belonged to us! I also saw the two beautiful, small vases that had been my grandmother's, but I did not get them back either. He threw us out of the house! I kept that one rug firmly tucked under my arm though, and to this day, it is always beside my bed.

Many people took advantage of the misery of others. The Dutch government bought paintings from Jews at a ridiculously low price, and after the liberation, offered to let surviving relatives buy them back at a very high price—with money they did not have. As well, it was almost impossible to prove that the property belonged to your family because all the family had been killed. So, still today (1999) those paintings are in the hands of the Dutch government. In April 1949, I received half of the amount of the Nazis' evaluation of my father's business when it was confiscated: It was valued at NLF 143,906.65; minus expenses, I received only NLF 69,084.66. Why I—as the sole survivor—received only half has never been clear to me.

In 1992, Jochebed and I also received Wiedergutmachung payments from the German Government as compensation for relatives we lost. I received NLF 5000-, and Jochebed received NLF 1000-. I could not prove that all my family members who were murdered in the gas chambers were dead and that I was the sole survivor. Otherwise, I could have received much more. As it was, I urged the payment of this compensation before I, too, died. They had already waited too long to compensate us.

In February 1943, when Jeantje was 4 weeks old, the few Jewish people who were left in Amsterdam, including us,

12 January, 1943. A plate made by Aat on the occasion of Jochebed's birth (here called Jeanne, because Rie's sister, Jeanne, had been taken by this time.

got a notice that we all had to move into the "ghetto." It was called 'Transvaalbuurt'—and it was located about 3 km south of the old Jewish quarter. A lot of Jews had moved there in the first decades of the 20th century. We got a one-room apartment in a house at Reitzstraat 34, I, on the second floor. The ghetto was a poor part of Amsterdam but not a bad part. A lot of Jews had lived there: Now all the Jews still in Amsterdam had to move there. The ghetto was blocked off by a chain. The streets had South African names like Krugerstraat. The apartment that we got was actually not too bad, and we were allowed to move with a moving van. As we were married in October 1940, our stuff was still quite new.

> **Author's Note:** *At this point in time, the Jews resided in three central areas of the city, which were separated by the canals. Each of these areas was turned into a distinct Jewish area, Judenviertel in German: in the east (**Transvaalbuurt**), in the south (Rivierenbuurt) and in the centre (**Waterlooplein, Nieuwmarkt**, and **Plantage**). The word ghetto gives the impression of a neighbourhood surrounded by walls with large iron gates, but this was not the case in Amsterdam: Rather, the 'walls' of the Judenviertels were the canals, and the 'gates' were the bridges, closed off by thick chains.*

I only had four cotton diapers for Jeantje, so during the day she lay on a mat on top of a dripping pan so that the little 'marbles' could fall through to the bottom. The diapers were saved for the night or when it was colder. We were there about two months. At that time, hoarding was forbidden for Jews. However, my neighbour gave me a lot of glass jars with preserved spinach and told me that I could keep all the jars.

Every night the green car arrived on the streets, and the Dutch police knocked on doors and took the Jews within the houses away. I didn't know many of my neighbours because they came from all over Amsterdam. Several times we had to show the police the exemption stamp. Once, when Elkan was ill with a heavy flu, the police told me that he had to go with them. He said firmly, "I am sick and I have a paper." They looked around, went into the bathroom, checked the cupboards and took whatever we had from the black market, like chocolates and such, put them in their pockets, and left.

At first, my parents were allowed to stay in their Rotterdam house because four other Jewish families were moved in with them. But eventually they went into hiding in their own house, and then came the day that they too were discovered, rounded up, and put on the train for Camp Westerbork. My great-aunts, Elisabeth and Duifje, were also picked up in Rotterdam and sent to Camp Westerbork. Elisabeth was gassed in Auschwitz on October 15, 1942, and Duifje was gassed there on October 19, 1942.

My parents were not immediately shipped on to the Polish camps because the Germans held them in Westerbork for several months. They were allowed to write once every two weeks, and we were allowed to send packages through the approved routes. A letter came from my father, asking me to please send some clothing for my mother. She didn't have anything anymore. My father had a strong personality and was very courageous, but my mother was totally depressed. Because I was in Amsterdam, I asked their neighbours in Rotterdam for help. They went to my parents' house and sent me two summer dresses for my mother. The rest had been confiscated.

I sent my parents all kinds of food and comforting letters. I once had a jar of delicious apricot jam, but I did not give it to them—I liked it too much myself. Much later, once I knew what had happened to them, I regretted it, and it weighed heavily on my conscience. However, I did send them homemade strawberry jam.

In the end I was totally out of wrapping paper or newspaper. I remember sitting in my chair with a pound of butter, which I wanted to send to my family, and I cried because I could no longer get wax paper—not from friends or from the office—so there was nothing to ship it in. I had to give up. My father must have thought, "My God, why doesn't she ship anything anymore?"

What, indeed, could Elkan and I do for my parents now? I found out after the war that they were shipped on the train to Sobibor where they were gassed on June 11, 1943. It was terrible.

CHAPTER 7

We are Rounded Up

Then came the time that they took Elkan and me and Jeantje. It was May 1943 and Jeantje was 4 months old. My parents were still in Camp Westerbork. There was a hammering on the door. All around us people were rounded up, and all our furniture and stuff was thrown out the windows. We saw it all happen.

Members of the NSB—the young ones, the rough guys—told us that we had to go as well. But I said, "No, no, no. We have a *Sperre*, so we don't have to go. We have a little baby. She is only eight weeks old, and you can't take us when the baby is only eight weeks old." But the guy looked at the wedding book (where you write down the births of your children) and said, "Oh, no, this baby is four months old. You are going with us."

So the three of us had to go with them. We had a little wicker basket, so we put Jeantje in it, with milk bottles, hot water bottles, and diapers. Full. Heavy. And then we had a little hand baggage. We had to go to the *Hollandse Schouwburg*, located at Plantage Middenlaan 24. This was a transit location. We were forced to take the baby across the street to the daycare centre, the *crèche*, and leave her there.

Author's Note: *Before the war, the Dutch Theatre (**Hollandsche Schouwburg**) was one of Amsterdam's most glittering theatres. During the Nazi Occupation, it was called the Joodse Schouwburg, the Jewish Theatre, because, for a time in 1941 and 1942, the Jews were permitted its use for their plays and concerts. However, starting in July 1942, the Nazis used the Schouwburg as a convenient assembly place for arrested Jews, out of sight of the citizens of Amsterdam. It was an ideal building for this purpose, as it had no windows on the street side.*

For some time, arrestees were taken both to the Central Station and the Schouwburg, but as procedures became more practised, arrestees were taken increasingly to the Schouwburg. Special cases, such as people whom the Germans wanted to process separately because of some transgression of regulations, continued to be taken to the Central Station to be put directly on trains. At both points, officials of the Jewish Council were present to keep order, to assist with screening, and to minister to the many needs of the people. In any given week, there could be as many as 400 Jews held in the Schouwburg, waiting for deportation to Camp Westerbork by sealed trains in the middle of the night.

At the entrance to the Schouwburg were some Jewish people who were forced to collaborate and work for the Germans. They told Elkan that they knew a way to get us out. We were told that there was an SS guard—Alphons Zündler was his name—who could be bribed and who was willing to turn his head in the other direction in order to let people go. Zündler was known

The daycare across from the Dutch Theatre.

to accept alcohol and also sex with Jewish women for their freedom. Elkan was wearing pants with lots of pockets that I had sewn into them. He had cash, gold rings, and diamonds (given to us by my grandfather) with him. I had filled a bag with black tea leaves, which was a rare commodity at the time. The idea was that the diamonds and gold were for greater favours, while tea leaves could be traded for smaller ones.

1941-1945. The Dutch Theatre.

Elkan approached Zündler and told him that we had a baby on the other side of the street who was only 3½ months old and we had to get out. While saying that, he discreetly drew Zündler's attention to the small handful of diamonds in his hand. Zündler accepted the offer—the second person who saved our lives.

Author's Note: Alfons Zündler (1919-1996) was the only member of the SS known to have ever accepted bribes from the Jews. In 1941, Zündler was wounded when shrapnel entered his right lung, and he was discharged from active service and sent to Amsterdam for "less physical" work. From the summer of 1942 to the spring of 1943, he was in charge of five SS guards administering the Hollandsche Schouwburg. He led roundups of Jews, transporting them from their houses to the theatre and from there to Camp Westerbork.

While working at the theatre, Zündler was said to have accepted bribes (sex, diamonds, alcohol, etc.) to allow the escape of a few Jews. However, in some cases he simply let Jews go without personal gain.

Late in 1943, Zündler and several other SS guards were arrested and imprisoned at Scheveningen and tried for *violation of Aryan racial laws by an SS court martial in The Hague. He was sentenced to death for **Rassenschande**, the Nazi term for sexual relations between Aryans and Jews, but later the sentence was commuted to ten years in Dachau. Two years into his sentence, in February 1945, he was released back into an SS division just as Nazi Germany was collapsing. He surrendered to the British army two months later, and was held as a British prisoner of war until 1946.*

1943 - Alfons Zundler, age 25.

In 1993, he was nominated for the Yad Vashem award with the title of "Righteous Among the Nations" that is given to non-Jewish rescuers of Jews. Twenty-three people affirmed that he had saved their lives at the Schouwburg, and others affirmed that he had let them escape during the roundups. He is known to have saved more than this, but some have never come forward, Rie and Elkan among them. His nomination for the title unsurprisingly led to controversy as many Dutch Jews claimed that he was motivated by sex, alcohol, or material gain. Early in 1994, after investigation, Yad Vashem decided against granting him the award. However, they wrote him a letter to thank him for the fact that he had saved several Jews from deportations. In January 1996, Alfons Zündler passed away in Munich, Germany.

(Lord Nobongo: De Personen Encyclopedie, February 20, 2005)

As the *crèche* (daycare) for the babies and children under 13 years old was on the opposite side of the street from the *Schouwburg*. The Chairman of the Jewish Council told me to go across the street to feed the baby her bottle. Zündler told Elkan that when the changing of the guard occurred, he would call over the intercom, "Mr. Katan, your baby is seriously ill. Please come at once." Elkan was then to run over to the crèche and we could escape.

That is exactly what happened. But it was not so easy to get out because there was a Jewish director of the nursery. Mrs. Pimentel absolutely refused to let us take our baby because she was responsible for her. She would be sent to the East if children registered at the nursery went missing. But we did not hesitate. It's incredible to me now, but we found our baby right away—even among forty or fifty babies. We picked her up, pushed past the director, and ran out.

Author's Note: Mrs. Pimentel had been the director of the daycare in Amsterdam since 1926. In 1942, the crèche or daycare, was taken over by the Germans and was used to house all of the arrested children under 13 years of age, whose parents were being kept in the Schouwburg across the street. In 1943, along with all but two of the staff at the daycare, Ms. Pimentel was sent to Auschwitz and died there.

A significant resistance movement operated inside the crèche, working to extract and save as many Jewish children as possible. Walter Süskind, a German Jewish refugee, compiled the lists of those to be deported. He removed the registration cards of children, making it possible for volunteer student groups to smuggle them out and put them in contact with different

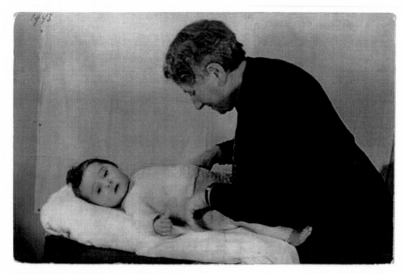

943. Mrs Pimenthal, Director of the Daycare.

Razzia (rounding-up) in Amsterdam.

The tram, blocking the view of the guards, offered chances to escape.

organizations, such as the Westerweel group. It is estimated that about 600 of the 5,000-6,000 children who passed through the crèche, were saved. At the height of its operations, from May to Sept. 1943, resistance workers may have saved up to 20 percent of the children. Babies were smuggled out in empty boxes or potato sacks. Later, when nurses were allowed to take babies outside, they went for walks but returned carrying large dolls.

I carried our baby in her basket, running down the street to the first corner. That was not easy because the basket was very heavy. When I turned the corner, I had to stop and catch my breath. One of the handles on the basket had broken, and in order to keep running and not drop the basket, I had to dig my fingers into a little ridge on the basket. But Elkan said, "You can't stop now. We can't stay here." So we ran into a Jewish grocery shop. The baby was crying all the time; I didn't know why, and I couldn't quiet her. The baby's nose was stuffed up, but we had not noticed. We asked the shopkeeper, who was Jewish, for warm water for the bottle and some water for us to drink. We were so tired.

Where to go? We walked all the way back to our apartment— it took about 40 minutes to get there. On the day we were rounded up and forced out of our apartment, Elkan had locked the special lock, which had been installed on his orders; it was a lock made by a locksmith, and only Elkan had the key. He had expected that the house would be pulsed, and that once the pulsers left, no one would be able to go back in again. So we carried the baby back to the house in the Reitzstraat and saw that the Nazis had sealed the lock with wax, but Elkan broke the seal and unlocked the door. What a relief. We were happy, at least temporarily, to be back in our own house, even though it was almost empty.

As soon as we escaped from the Hollandse Schouwburg, we knew that we had to go into hiding and that we could not take Jeantje, our baby, with us. We would have to give her away.

Immediately we thought of Mr. van de Bunt. Elkan used to work for the firm of van de Bunt and Starreveld. Mr. van de Bunt had always said that when the baby was born and we needed to go into hiding, we could call on him. He lived in Bloemendaal, near the beach. He was the head of the Red Cross there and hid other people as well. He said he knew of a way to hide the baby with a non-Jewish family, through a judge who had promised to provide false identity papers for Jewish babies.

Author's Note: *In January 1942, a Jewish baby boy, three weeks old, was found on the doorstep of a non-Jewish Dutch judge. He was very concerned about it and did not know what to do with the baby. He invited eleven friends, who were all judges, to come to his house and suggested that they provide non-Jewish identity papers to save Jewish babies. They could appropriate the names of persons who had disappeared in the bombing of Rotterdam in May 1940, and give the children identification papers that could not be traced back to living people. Through official court channels, approximately sixty Dutch Jewish babies thereby received false papers.*

Now we knew we had to give our baby away—a terrible, agonizing decision for us both. Mr. van de Bunt told us that a woman would come to pick Jeantje up. We were not to speak to the woman—just hand her a piece of paper with instructions for the care of the baby. It was actually Mrs. van de Bunt who came to pick up the baby, but we didn't know that at the time. I gave my baby away with a little note to this woman, whom I had never met before. It was terrible to give my baby away, but I was so grateful that we had such wonderful people to turn to when our very lives were at stake. What if Mr. and Mrs. van de Bunt had not taken our baby into hiding? What if the judge had not organized false papers for Jewish babies? Would they be kind to Jeantje? Would she survive? It would be more than two years before we found out.

The diamonds had tempted Zündler. Elkan had shown great

initiative in bribing Zündler, and in putting that special lock on our apartment. We had gripped our courage in both hands and run away. Luck was certainly with us, for the baby didn't cry very hard as we ran away. But all good fortunes were not enough to save us. This was a time when there were many Dutch people who didn't care what happened to the Jews and many who handed them over to the Germans. But we were helped by Dutch people who risked their lives to help us. But would it be enough? Would Elkan and I be able to go into hiding?

We knew we had to go into hiding quickly, but we didn't know anyone who could hide us. Then we remembered Mr. J. A. Bruinhout, who rented a small house that my father owned. My father had always said that if we were in trouble, we should go to him. He was a family friend who lived in Schiebroek, near Rotterdam. I contacted him, and he told us he knew somebody in the province of Drenthe in North-east Holland who could help us. He told us that Drenthe is quite a Christian area, and he gave us the name of a man who sold school books to Christian schools. This man would be able to help us escape from Amsterdam. He mailed us an address in Emmer-Compascuum, which is in a very rural area of southeast Drenthe. I repeated the word Emmer-Compascuum 200 times to remember where we had to go, and we wrote it down on a little sliver of paper and put it under the carpet. It was a very poor district of Holland, where they dug peat. It had lots and lots of canals, and it was not far from Camp Westerbork and not far from the German border. What would we have done without Mr. Bruinhout?

We knew that we needed false identity papers with no "J" on them because we had to get out of Amsterdam. Earlier, we couldn't ride the trains with our Jewish identity papers. We had given our false identity papers away when it was relatively easy to get them; now it was much more difficult to get them. Where would we get them now? Once again, someone was willing to help us. Elkan got in touch with one of his co-workers, a young man about 22 years of age, very tall and blonde like a German, who told Elkan that he knew a group of Communists who were producing false identity papers. I am so sorry now that I cannot remember the young man's name. He offered to take us there: It was a long walk to southeast Amsterdam, but well worth it. These people were able to produce false identity papers for us. They took my photo and put it on my new identity card with the name, Hendrika de Bruin; Elkan's new name was Huub Jacobs.

Next, the young man took us to his mother's house, hoping that she would be willing to take us in for the night. It was about a 90-minute walk to the far east of Amsterdam. But his mother would not help us; she wouldn't even come outside her house but shouted through the window that she had heard that if you have Jews in the house, the Nazis will shoot you. This was a typical attitude in Holland at that time. Everyone was frightened of the Nazis, and everyone felt their lives were threatened every day. They couldn't risk their family's lives for people they didn't know, let alone for Jews. But this made us extra grateful to her son, who was willing to risk his life helping us.

What would we do now? We had no choice. We went back to our apartment, which was very risky. The young man met us the next day to help us get out of Amsterdam by train. We could not go alone to southeast Drenthe by train, for the Amsterdam station was filled with NSB members and Germans, six rows deep, waiting to catch Jewish people fleeing from Amsterdam. Our young blond friend told us that he could get us through and out of Amsterdam: He was very clever. When we arrived at the train station, there were thousands of people there, and he leaned forward impatiently past us and handed his own identity papers to the German guard— and we were in. He accompanied us on the train until we reached Zwolle, 120 km. north of Amsterdam, where we had to change trains. We had to disembark, not only to change trains but also to eat. We went to the Geitenberg Hotel opposite the train station where there were many Germans having lunch, but the young man told us to relax, sit quietly, and eat something. We were no longer wearing the yellow "J" on our clothes, so no one looked at us. Our friend told us that he would put us on the right train for Emmen, but then we would have to go on alone because he had to return to Amsterdam. He did all this for us without fuss, yet every moment we could have been discovered, and he would have been beaten and probably shipped off to the labour camps. He was another essential helper who quietly risked his life for a Jewish couple.

We sat quietly in the train compartment until we reached Emmen, where we had to get off to go to Emmer-Compascuum, which is a tiny dot on the map. It is located in the middle of meadows, potato fields, and flatlands with some scattered farmhouses.

It was not easy to get off the train because a local soccer team wanted to get on. The train left, and we stood alone in the dark each with two small suitcases, just the two of us, waiting to be collected—alone on the platform of the little station, lit with only one little lamp. We waited a full hour. We had no option but to trust that the people who were going to hide us would not abandon us. I had never been afraid during all the war years, but this was the worst hour I had ever spent. We didn't know what to do, for there was no hiding place in those flat fields, and no one we knew or could trust. Would we survive?

> **Author's Note:** *Out of a population of 140,000 Jews, about 22,000 chose to hide – **onderduiken** – or submerge. Most went into hiding on their own or as couples. Parents had to separate from their children; as terrible as this was, it was necessary if the children were to have a chance to live. The 'onderduikers' usually had no support group of any kind, which meant that those in hiding could no longer receive food rations. Almost half of them were ultimately captured.*
>
> *Hiding Jews in Holland was not a capital offence, as it was in*

Poland. However, Dutch people who hid Jews were threatened with being sent to concentration camps, and many did end up in the camps. Despite this threat, some people were willing to shelter Jews in exchange for money and ration coupons. Many others were not so mercenary, and willing to help purely out of mercy; many of these were devout Christians. In southern Drenthe, the people who hid fugitives or helped in one way or another were nearly all **Gereformeerden** *(orthodox Calvinists). They were probably responsible for helping 25 percent of all the Dutch Jews who went underground. In the southern provinces of Brabant and Limburg, Roman Catholic communities similarly developed networks to save Jews.*

CHAPTER 8

The Middel Farm

Then someone came. Farmer Middel and another man arrived on bikes and they had two bikes for us. My bike was too high for me, and I was already exhausted; nonetheless, we had to bike through the darkness more than 15 km. The farm was on a canal, and there was a private bridge that turned to let boats through. We were taken up to the Middel's large attic, which was where they were going to hide us. This attic had a thin wooden floor, so that everyone downstairs would be able to hear every step we took. It was very very sparse: There was a mattress on the floor stuffed with oats— very hard, but we got used to it, and we had two wooden crates to sit on. There were hundreds of mice. There were so many mice that if we put our plates down, the mice would steal the food. Farmer Middel brought us a little cat, but the cat was more afraid of the mice than they were of him.

Because we were in hiding, the Middels could not get food coupons from the government for us. They would have to find the food another way. We paid a lot of money for our food and lodging. The Middels were taking a risk hiding us, but they were also poor farmers making money off of us. We were grateful that they were hiding us, but it was difficult because they so clearly regarded us as a source of income. Every morning, Mrs. Middel brought us dark rye bread, which she had baked herself, with sugar syrup to put on top of the bread. In the evenings, we got a lot of potatoes and a tiny little bit of meat. When Mr. Middel came up the stairs, he always tried to get a look at my naked shoulders, so I cowered deep under the blanket. After a while, the Middels were not kind to us. They brought up bowls of a kind of spinach (*snijbiet*) with no potatoes or meat and two glasses of milk. Mrs. Middel began to come upstairs sometimes to look into the toilet bucket to make sure that we had not thrown our food into it. The food was a distraction, but it was still really bad. There was a large bucket for a toilet, and once a week we got a jug of hot water and a skimpy towel to wash ourselves. I could hardly ever wash my hair. We got water for drinking, but hardly any other water for washing.

Then Farmer Middel asked for more money, even though we already had given him a great deal. Elkan wrote a letter to Mr. Bruinhout to ask him to send some money. Mr. Bruinhout actually brought the money to us in person—he was very kind— and handed over 500 guilders (equivalent to 500 dollars today) to Elkan. This was a lot of money. Unfortunately, he gave Elkan the money in plain sight of Farmer Middel and his wife. When they saw the money, they looked at each other most meaningfully.

The next day, Elkan asked if he could buy some meat. Farmer Middel actually told him that it would cost 500 guilders for one goat. Now, in the North of Holland, a goat is the cheapest thing that you can buy. There in the shed was a white goat, just an ordinary goat with a beard—certainly not worth 500 guilders. It was a crazy price for a goat. The Middels were just putting Elkan's money in their pockets. There were plenty of goats there. Farmer Middel slaughtered the goat himself. We had come from the city, and I didn't want to watch the slaughter. Next morning we were invited to the shed. I was too squeamish to even look at the animal that I had seen walking around just the day before. Elkan reminded me that I had seen meat hanging in the butcher shop in the city.

The goat was duly cooked and roasted. That first night, we got potatoes, a little bit of vegetables, and the liver of the goat, for the farmer thought that Jewish people like to eat liver. We did like it very much because it had the taste of calf's liver. The next day, however, we only got a little piece of the meat of that goat. Every night we could smell the meat they were frying and roasting, but we got none of it upstairs. What could we do? This goat was so terribly expensive – 500 Dutch guilders, which in that time was a fortune. There were so many other goats around too, but we hardly got a single piece of meat.

When we asked Farmer Middel for some meat, he told us that the 500 guilders were now gone, and they didn't have any more money to buy meat. If we wanted to stay with him, it would cost us more money. We were very worried that we would run out of money. If we ran out of money, would they just turn us out into the night? It was such a difficult time.

Then came the night that we had to come down and kneel for an hour in a crawl space with cobwebs, as Mrs. Middel was so afraid that the Nazis were snooping around. The Germans threatened anyone who hid the Jews with concentration camp. She had heard all kinds of horror stories and she insisted that Mr. Middel close the turning bridge. Nothing happened that night, but the Middels decided that we had to leave. We could only hope that they would find us another place. Our fate was looking pretty bleak, but we reminded ourselves that we were not yet in Camp Westerbork.

CHAPTER 9

The Pepping Family

The next day, Mr. Pepping came to us in our attic and brought us to his family. It seemed as if it was a long way away from the Middel farm because the farmer's cart moved so slowly. I don't know how far it actually was because the whole area was unfamiliar to us. Naturally we had never been allowed to explore the area, and we had arrived after dark. The Peppings had a nicer house that was not a farmhouse. Mr. Pepping was a carpenter, his wife was a very nice young woman, and they had a 3-year-old little boy. We were taken upstairs to a little room about 3m by 4m. The room was almost totally empty. There was a narrow bed, 80 cm. wide, for one person. There were three crates—two to sit on and one for the table. There was a bucket with a lid on top in the corner for a toilet, and that was it. The room was on the south side so that when the sun was shining we had to close the shutters.

By this time, we had been in hiding for quite some time. We were safe, but oh, God, what did we have to do? We were shut up in that little room for month after month and there was nothing to do. We asked for a book or a newspaper, but because the Peppings were illiterate, it would attract attention if they asked for a newspaper in the village. Once they did get a newspaper, but it was all about the NSB and was called the newspaper of the North. We soon got sick of it, of course. We asked if we could get some writing paper to mail a letter out, which we got once. Everything was impossible. The woman of the house was really a sweetheart. She could not hang our wash outside because the neighbours would see it. She did her best, but her husband was not so nice.

One day we got a set of playing cards so we played canasta. We decided that I would teach Elkan about being a pharmacist and Elkan would teach me about accountancy. I suggested that Elkan might work on his doctorate, but without books it was impossible. However, we were young, still very much in love, and happy in each other's company. We talked a lot, we slept a lot—we did sleep a lot. A whole year is a long, long time in a very small room. So many marriages broke up because of this close proximity with nothing to do. For us, it actually made our marriage stronger—we had a very good marriage, believe me.

We saw all the German planes coming over, and I put little marks on the wall. It was impossible to keep count because there were so many of them. These planes were flying over Drenthe and Groningen in the north, heading back to Germany.

But then the Peppings had another child. When the baby was born, we couldn't stay there any longer because they needed our room. We were also afraid that people would come over to the house to see the new baby. The couple's little boy, who was about 4 or 4 ½, never came near our door because he didn't know we were there.

CHAPTER 10

The Schuitema Families

There seemed to be some kind of network amongst these people. When one family could not keep us, they arranged for another family to take us in. Naturally, we never found out how they organized things, who the leaders were, and whether they were hiding other Jews, too. It would be too dangerous to tell us these things as they could be forced out of us if we were rounded up. Every one of the families who took us in was essential to our survival; we were completely dependent upon their goodwill. They must have had to live a most secretive life. There must have been threats that we knew nothing about from inquisitive neighbours or collaborators who would collect 40 guilders from the Germans for turning us in. Each family was different too, and had different motives for hiding us.

When Mr. Pepping could not hide us any longer, he took us over to Wessel and Tina Schuitema. This was a very Christian, very religious couple. He was slim with a beard and long hair and very welcoming. He looked just like the pictures of Jesus. He said, "Whoever is in trouble may come to me. We will help them." He was the organist in the church, and she was a preacher. They read the Bible three times a day at the kitchen table, and they would pray. With their big Bible, they tried to convert us to Christianity. He first showed me from the Bible how the Jews were chased out of Jerusalem by the Romans and told us that we would be punished forever.

This family was very good to us. They were really fine, good people. We were given a little bedroom on one side of the house, and we could actually move around a little bit there. I made all the beds for the family and was allowed to do some cleaning too. Tina didn't like housecleaning, so I was happy to help. We were never allowed to go outside in the daytime, but with this family we could go outside for fifteen minutes every night when it was very dark—when there was no moon, of course. So we had some fresh air, which was a big improvement. There was a piano in the house, and as both of us could play, we were allowed to play it. Sometimes I would help with the mending and the darning of socks.

This family was so Christian that they could not lie. Tina was a little worried about what she would say if somebody knocked on the door and asked who we were. We decided that we would tell them that I was a cousin from Rotterdam, who had left because of the bombardment. I had come to their place because life was good here in the Northeast.

But, once again, we had to move. This time we were brought to their parents' house—Sjoerd and Fennechien Schuitema. They were also very fine people; they treated us even better. Sjoerd was a schoolteacher, and Fennechien was a very warm, fine person. They did everything they could for us, but we had to be in a little room upstairs again. And again, we had nothing to do. Every night at 10:00, however, we were allowed to go downstairs and listen to the news on the radio. One day we heard that the Allied forces were advancing through Italy.

In the little room upstairs, we slept in a bed in a cupboard. It was very short – too short for Elkan. We slept close to each other, like a pretzel. Under the bed was a drawer, with a slaughtered, pickled pig stored in it. It was stored there until the winter when it would be eaten. We couldn't smell it, but it was there. We also had our very own little radio. We could listen to Radio Oranje, the Dutch radio broadcasts from London, England, and this kept us up-to-date with all the news. One hour a day we could hear the radio. We were so happy to have this.

1944 - Sjoerd and Fennechien Schuitema

Their daughter, Fennie, was still at home. Fennie was a nurse working in an old-age home. She was very very good to us. That was the start of good eating: They served us pea or carrot soup, meat, and potatoes and vegetables from their own garden. So I started to gain weight. When I didn't eat it, she was offended, so I had to eat it. She took such care of us. My husband was slim and he didn't gain weight. I had some camisoles, and I had to re-knit them so that they would fit. There was no possibility of buying anything. Mrs. Schuitema admired my knitting, and so she brought me wool to knit socks for her girl. I had never knit socks before—I made so many mistakes. And then she let us clean the whole attic. People were not always very nice in the war, but this lady was very nice to us. We didn't have to pay much money, either. We only had to pay for what we ate, and that was very nice. In the evenings, if it was dark, we were allowed to go walking outside in the garden with Fennie.

CHAPTER 11

The van Seijen Family

But we could not stay at the Schuitema's house very long. We learned that we were going to be moved back to the Pepping family when the Pepping baby was old enough. But then a terrible tragedy occurred. I remember very clearly that, when the baby was 3-months old, the mother put her baby out in her baby carriage in the hot sun, with the carriage hood up. The little baby died from the heat. We saw through a slit in the curtain the funeral procession from our upstairs room. The mother looked so sad, so very very sad. She had to walk alone, all dressed in black, in front of the procession with all the people from the village following behind her. Her husband was not walking with her—she walked on her own, alone. How terrible. How terrible.

After the death of the Pepping baby, we wondered what would become of us. Were there more people in this part of Holland willing to help two adult Jews? Indeed, there were. We were taken to stay with the family of Bep and Jan van Seijen. They had two little daughters, Corrie and Riekje. When we arrived, the children were about 7 and 2, and Bep was expecting another baby. Like us, they were from Rotterdam. This couple was very compassionate and friendly to us, and he was very anti-German. We were not the first or only people that they hid; they had hidden many others. It had been Bep's decision to take us. Jan knew that he would be away during the week, and it would be mainly Bep who would be looking after us.

We were given two little rooms upstairs, one to sleep in and one to sit in. The small sitting

Jan and Bep van Seijen with Corrie and Riekje.

room had two chairs and a little table. We were allowed to come downstairs and help around the house, and help with the children. In the evenings, when all the windows were covered with black paper (a must for all the houses in the Netherlands), we could come down into the sitting room. They were poor, but they never accepted more from us than they needed to pay for our food.

We became almost part of the family—a secret part. Two-year-old Riekje, born in 1941, would jump into bed with us each morning. Corrie was much older and had to be warned not to tell

Houses of the van Seijen and Schuitema families in Emmen-Compascum.

Artwork made by Elkan while in hiding.

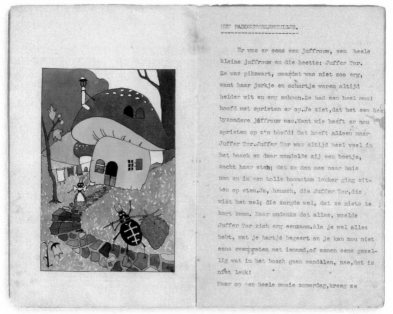

1944 - A present for Corrie van Seijen's ninth birthday made by Rie and Elkan while they were in hiding.

anyone that we were living with them. Corrie kept that secret and never told anyone. What a remarkable little girl she was. Corrie really understood how serious this matter was. She was very bright and was in first grade when we were there. One day Corrie had to do arithmetic with numbers over ten, so she asked Elkan for help. She was delighted when he suggested that she use her toes to calculate as well. Every day at lunchtime, Corrie climbed the stairs twice in order to carry the excellent hot food that Bep made for us—one plate at a time. We decided to make a special present for Corrie for her seventh birthday. We made a little book for her. It was called Het Paddestoelen-huisje (The Little Mushroom House), and Elkan did all the illustrations. Elkan actually spent a great deal of his time sketching and drawing.

One day there was a fire behind the van Seijen house, in a shed that housed their pig, as well as coal and wood for burning fires. The firemen put their hoses right next to the house, which frightened Corrie. This was a dangerous day for us, and we had to keep very quiet.

There was other work for us to do as well. Regularly, a little boat, loaded with blocks of peat to use as fuel, arrived, and it was the job of those in hiding, including Elkan, to unload the boat. Sometimes when there was no moon in the sky, Elkan could get out of the house to go to the nearby soccer field and sit on a little shed.

Jan van Seijen hated the Germans, and so did his neighbour! When the Allied planes flew over the house, this neighbour would run outside and shout, "Throw it all "kaput" on the dirty Nazis." We kept telling him to be quiet and stop doing this because it was too dangerous.

At Easter in 1944, they served a big dinner. They cooked all their meals on a stove fueled by peat. A brother came over and slaughtered a rabbit. But they knew that we didn't eat rabbit, so Bep prepared a chicken for us. This was so sensitive of her. Jan said, "There is only one thing that's missing at this table—the matzos." I was moved to tears by this and remembered it always. After that wonderful Easter meal, we gave Jan and Bep a thank you card. One side had an image of Queen Wilhelmina and the other had a note from Elkan: "In remembrance of very pleasant Easter days in difficult times." It was signed by us both and dated April 1944.

CHAPTER 12

Betrayed

We had a very good safe place with the van Seijens, so trustful and filled with love, but it became too dangerous for us there. They never told us too many details, but we were moved back to Wessel and Tina Schuitema's house. But it was not safe there, either. In the days following Mad Tuesday (Dolle Dinsdag), Sept. 5, 1944, there were a great many members of the NSB in Drenthe. On Dolle Dinsdag many of the NSB fled from the West to Groningen, and many came close to the Schuitema's house. So this was a very dangerous area for Jewish men to be hiding; women had more of a chance at survival.

Author's Note: *September 5, 1944 was called Mad Tuesday (**Dolle Dinsdag**), because of the chaos caused when the BBC mistakenly reported that the city of Breda in southern Holland had been liberated. Many people celebrated, since they thought their liberation would soon be at hand. At the same time, many Germans and Dutch NSB-ers (see next note) began fleeing toward the German border, destroying documents as they went. It was a day of great shame for the Dutch Nazis. As the last phases of the deportations began, more 'Jew-*

hunters' were drafted in to assist. These were mainly Dutch anti-Semites, joined by a certain number of Dutch policemen. They spread out into the countryside, working to earn the bounty of 40 guilders for each Jew they apprehended.

And so it happened. In the evening of January 2, 1945, I heard a whole crowd of people, and, looking under the curtain out the window, I saw 10 *Landwachters*, the Home Guard that rounded up the Jews. We had been in bed, so Elkan grabbed all his clothes and hid in the little cupboard that had been built behind the wall just in case. Only one person could fit in there. I had insisted that if something happened, it would be Elkan who went into that cupboard. I hoped that I would be able to save myself. Elkan didn't want it to be that way, but that was the deal. The reason for this was that Jewish men found in hiding, especially at the end of the war, would be immediately shot.

Author's Note: *Nationaal-Socialistische Beweging, the National Socialist Movement, was the Dutch wing of the International Fascist movement, which was the only legal political party that had been operating in the Netherlands from 1931 until the liberation in May 1945. It was known to all as the NSB. During WWII, it was the only legal political party, having a membership in 1940 of about 100,000. In the beginning of 1943, many male members of the NSB were organized as part of the* **Landwacht***, or Home Guard, who assisted the government in controlling the population. Amongst their duties was the apprehension of Jews in hiding.*

The police knocked on the house door and loudly demanded that Mrs. Schuitema hand over the Jews who she was hiding. She kept insisting that there were no Jews in her house, but they didn't listen to her and burst into the house. The police looked around the downstairs and then came upstairs and found me in bed. They asked me who I was. I told them I was a niece from Rotterdam, just visiting. Just then, however, I spied one of Elkan's sock garters lying on the floor. One of the NSB members ordered me to get out of bed. He said, "Maybe your husband is here as well." He had a karrawats (a stiff whip for torturing) in his boot. I told him that they had better leave the room so that I could get dressed. They did not leave the room, but one man turned his face to the window and the other turned his face to the wall. While I was under the blankets putting on my clothes, I quickly grabbed the sock garter and pulled it under the blanket. Oh, I thanked God that I had that sock garter hidden. Ah, that garter, it still burns in my head because only men wore sock garters; women did not wear them.

I had to get out of bed, go downstairs, and go outside. In that time, we had no leather for shoes, so we used wood to make the soles—small wooden strips. It was the second of January and it was so icy, I almost fell with every step I took. I was taken outside and shoved into the middle of a circle of NSB members and policemen. I put my hands on my hips and said, "Wow, you have the catch of the day. What a catch. One fat young woman!" I had had no exercise for the last two years, and even in the circumstances, we had been fed extremely well. I wore the dress that I had knitted for myself in Amsterdam. A client of Elkan's had given me 12 skeins of dark blue wool every time he came to visit. I had knitted a little coat and other baby things for my baby, and also a dress for myself. It was the only dress I had, and I didn't fit into it very well any more. When I got married, I had weighed 47 kg. (103 lbs.), but by then I weighed at least 63 kg. (139 lbs).

The policemen had expected me to be afraid and shy, but I was not panic-stricken at all. Thank God, Elkan stayed in the closet. They ordered me to walk to Emmen, which was the nearest town, 7 km. away. I couldn't do it after being inside for 2 years with no exercise. One of them suggested a bicycle. It was too high—most people were taller than me. Nevertheless, I had to ride that bike all the way to the police station in Emmen. It was cold and windy, biking along the icy roads near the canals. They had rounded up Jan van Seijen and Wessel Schuitema as well, and they made us all bike that distance in the cold.

When we arrived at the police station, they put me in a cell. I learned that they had rounded up almost all the men who had sheltered Elkan and me: Farmer Middel, Wessel Schuitema, and Jan van Seijen. I had to show my false identity papers, with the name of Hendrika de Bruin. (Elkan and I had practised writing our false signatures a thousand times.) I had to reproduce that signature then. You can write the "H" in so many ways—a thousand ways— with loops and straight and so on. But my hands were ice-cold as I had no gloves: They were red and swollen, and I was so exhausted after the bike ride that I couldn't reproduce the signature. The older NSB member asked me to try again twice more. But I couldn't reproduce that signature. Wessel Schuitema called out from his jail cell, "Aunt Rie. You can tell them everything. We have been betrayed." But I thought not; I was not going to say a word. He was right, though: We had been betrayed.

In the interrogation room, there was an officer, dressed like a gentleman in a very nice suit. There was also a woman sitting there, in black shoes, black stockings, and a set, determined face. She was the wife of an NSB collaborator. I found out after the war that she was Grietje Lamijer, a neighbour of the van Seijen's. Her husband was a tailor. She had seen me through the kitchen window, bathing Corrie in the sink, and she had been watching us as we moved from one house to the next. After the war, Jan van Seijen took her to court for her betrayal and collaboration with the Nazis. She declared that it was her duty to tell the militia that Jan van Seijen had Jews in his house and that those Jews had also been at Schuitema's house. On January 17, 1947, the local newspaper *Asser Courant* reported that she was sentenced to two years of prison for her collaboration—this was not long enough—and a lifetime deprivation of voting rights.

The officer in the jail, who seemed to be a lawyer, asked me my name, and I told him my new name and the story that we had planned. He didn't believe me. Mrs. Lameijer was listening, and she told him nervously that I was no cousin. After a long time of questioning, he caught me out in a lie, and I admitted my name was Marie van Daelen. I told him my husband had climbed out of the window when they changed the position of the guards. It was all a lie: I didn't know I could lie so well.

I was put in another room, and a policeman held a revolver to my breast. I told him to put that thing away and said, "You're not allowed to shoot me!"

And he put it away. I could hardly believe it. Sometimes you can't believe how you will behave when it is necessary. When I had to sit on a chair in the police cell, my blue woolen dress slid up too high, and one of the policemen scolded me for sitting so indecently. But I could not pull it down—I was too big and it didn't fit me very well. It seemed like a long time that I had to stay in a cell there. I got two slices of bread from a policeman, as well as two slices of his portion. He gave me this extra food—he was not a bad man. I remember him as another example of kindness amidst the horrors of war.

Then, from the police station in Emmen, I was brought by jeep to the jail in Assen. It was good to be outside and see the world again. But the people in that Assen jail were in terrible shape, all war victims, all very afraid of what would happen next. They were kicked everywhere and humiliated and then sent to Camp Westerbork. I shared a cell with a young woman and her baby, who was just beginning to walk. In the cell there was only one wooden bed, which we all had to share. That was terrible. In the door was a small peephole. But the policemen were very good to the child, and brought her milk and other food. Even in the Assen jail, I was reminded how kind people can be and how caring were the friends who had hidden us. Fennie Schuitema remembered that I was just about to have one of my terribly heavy periods, and she biked all the way to Assen to bring me a packet of feminine napkins; she gave them to the guards at the jail to give to me. I thanked God so fervently for Fennie and her thoughtfulness. Every woman can imagine how humiliating it would have been to cope with my periods in a jail cell without feminine napkins.

I got an infection around my nail—strange—I never had that before. It hurt, and I had to go to a doctor. As I was waiting next to a soldier and his young 18-year-old prisoner, the young man whispered to me, "I am planning to escape." I could see that there were German soldiers everywhere: high-ranking officers in green uniforms and green caps with silver plaques on the front. I knew it was impossible for me to escape: Even if I did run, where would I go? The young man didn't escape either.

So I had to give up and was returned to the cell, where I stayed for a few days. They planned to transfer me to another cell that already held six men. I told them firmly, "That I will not do." The police understood, and instead, I was given a thin mattress on the floor next to the desk of the old janitor. He had a long list on his desk with names on it, and during a conversation with him, I asked him to show me the list of the other people in the Assen jail. I was looking for the name "Huib", which was Elkan's hiding name, and it was not there. How good it was to know that. In the middle of the night, the old man began to touch my body. I kicked him, exclaiming, "What do you think you're doing?" I spent the rest of that night sitting on a chair.

CHAPTER 13

Camp Westerbork

On January 9th, 1945, my captors took me from Assen to Camp Westerbork, which was 15 minutes away. I enjoyed that trip in the open jeep so much. It was so beautiful—fresh air, houses, the moor, purple heather, green trees, etc. It had been so long since I had seen such beauty. Of course, I was very worried about Elkan, but I knew that I really must concentrate upon myself.

I didn't really know the significance of Camp Westerbork then because we had been in hiding when my family was shipped from Westerbork to their deaths in the east. When we were in hiding, we were very isolated from the progress of the war.

Author's Note: *From July 1942 until September 3, 1944, the Germans deported almost 100,000 Jews from Camp Westerbork: about 55,000 were sent to Auschwitz in 68 transport trains, about 35,000 to Sobibor in 19 trains, close to 5,000 to the Theresienstadt ghetto in 7 trains, and nearly 4,000 to the Bergen-Belsen concentration camp in 9 trains. Most of those deported to Auschwitz and Sobibor were killed upon arrival.*

(United States Holocaust Memorial Museum)

It was lucky for me that I arrived alone, for normally about 20 people arrived at the camp together. Instead of being thrown into one of the large barracks crowded with many people, I was put into an elite building with only 12 women. The wives of the Dutch Jewish elite lived here; for instance, there was the wife of the owner of Vroom and Dreesman, which was, and still is, a chain of Dutch

LAGER WESTERBORK

ARBEITSKARTE
ARBEIDSKAART

Katan-v.Dalen

Maria

Geb. 1o.7.15   Bar. 11

Gruppe
Groep   Nähstube

WESTERBORK,   1o.1.45   194

Rie's ID card from Camp Westerbork.

department stores founded in 1887 by brothers-in-law, Willem Vroom and Anton Dreesmann. I had so much luck as they were all intelligent, well-educated women. They were very good to me: They gave me a bedspread for a blanket, a precious, small piece of soap, and a small bedside table without a lock. I had arrived with nothing—only an infected finger, my under-sized woolen dress, and my coat.

This was a critical time in the war. At the order of the Allies, the Dutch train drivers had gone on strike, refusing to drive any more trains. Therefore, no more trains were transporting Jews to the death camps in the east. Mrs. Dreesman, a kind Catholic woman, told me, "You don't need to worry here. It is safe. The last train has departed. The management is now in the hands of Jews. Before they shipped the last people on the trains, the Germans selected 1000 people to be left behind to look after the running of the camp." Of course, the guards were all German.

Author's Note: *Hoping to weaken the German ability to move troops through the Netherlands, the Dutch government in London called for a national railway strike in September of*

1944. Almost all of the 30, 000 workers went into hiding, and the strike lasted for more than seven months. The Germans effected no reprisals; instead, they brought 4,000 to 5,000 railway men from Germany, who dealt solely with the needs of the German army: troop movements and the transport of supplies and food. From that time on, it was no longer possible for the Germans to use trains to ship the few remaining Jews in Camp Westerbork to the east.

In retaliation for the strike, Seyss-Inquart halted all barges and ships. As a result, the three largest cities in western Holland (Amsterdam, Rotterdam, and The Hague) lived on the brink of starvation throughout the frigid winter of 1944-45.

A lady came, and I had to follow her to the clothing department where there was so much stuff. I got a pair of wooden shoes: I could not walk in them at first, as I had no experience whatsoever in wearing wooden shoes, not coming from a farming family. I got brand new overalls too. The people in my building were a little suspicious because I had soap and these overalls. I think they suspected I was from the wrong side. But I told them who I was, and eventually they trusted me.

As my finger was so heavily infected, I could not work like everybody else. A doctor in Westerbork, who had been a heart specialist in peacetime, cut the finger to drain it. I was horribly ill. He told me not to work for a week, and then to come back to him. Everyone told me not to go out of the building during this time because all the German guards were there.

I hadn't expected to know anyone in Westerbork, but suddenly I heard Elkan's name. A blond young man of about twenty years old was asking if the wife of Elkan Katan was here. He was Elkan's cousin, Simon den Hartogh, Aunt Kiek's son. They had lived in The Hague before the war; I had seen him when I was eleven years old and he was maybe six but had not seen him since. He told me that he had been in the camp for a long time. His uncle was a very famous doctor, Coen van Emde Boas, professor of sexology. Under his uncle's sponsorship, Simon had acquired the papers to keep him in Westerbork as a carpenter.

I seized the opportunity and asked Simon for a lock for my little night table. Simon wasn't optimistic; he told me he had already stolen so many locks. That night, though, he came in with a lock. I could now put my soap in the cupboard. Anything you left unlocked was stolen—no one was a real thief, but no one had anything. I was so happy with the lock.

When my finger was healed, I had to go to the kitchen to peel potatoes all day. I had suffered carpal tunnel syndrome in the pharmacy from folding medication papers, and the first night after peeling potatoes, my wrist became painful again, and I knew that I couldn't do that work anymore. I told the Jewish woman in charge of the kitchen that I couldn't peel potatoes all day. She insisted, but I refused. I sat there for three days without peeling potatoes. She complained to the Jewish management, who told her to ask me what I wanted to do. I told them that I would like to go to the sewing workshop. I had never had a needle in my hand, but I thought that, after the war, if I could find my child, it would be wise to learn a bit here.

The sewing room was a very large hall with 30 or 40 women, and each was a specialist. This was how they had managed to be exempted from the deportation lists. One person made the gloves, another person made the bras, another made the shirts, and another made cuffs for clothing (all for the Nazis). As I did not have any clothes other than the dress I had on, I started to talk with everybody there. Mrs.

Deewee shoe cream poster hanging in Camp Westerbork. The cream was made by the van Daelen & van Wessel company.

Veltman made another bra for me and other articles of clothing that I needed. I watched the woman who made shirts and borders, and I learned a lot. There was also a large knitting-machine there, manned by a gentleman, Mr. Kattenburg, who made beautiful woolen socks for the Nazis. I promised myself that after the war I would get a knitting machine—and I did.

They asked me if I could work a hand-operated sewing machine. I told them that I could because my mother had one at home. It was explained to me how the machine worked, and I had to do mending—patching pants, repairing socks. This was all repair work for the people in the camp because for the more advanced work, there were very good specialized tailors there. Mrs. Pisk, a German Jewish woman, was the manager, and she was not easy to work for. She had been there for six years. Later, I asked to use one of the many pedal-operated sewing machines. That went much faster, and I managed to mend a big hamper of clothing in one day, which was an achievement. I had to sew *kippot* with a little button on the top, made out of six triangles; I sewed collars onto shirts, and I had to make gloves and bras. Not that I can still make them now, but I remember a lot about it. After awhile, Mrs. Pisk selected me to work in the button department, and I had to sort all the loose buttons, in order to sew them onto little cards. When Mrs. Pisk left the room, I let all the ladies in the room take all the buttons they wanted. I knew that they were all stolen anyway. Mrs. Pisk later went to Australia and worked in *haute couture*.

On the 11th of March, at 8:30 a.m., I was told to report to Herrn Wolff, the director at the central labour office, in barracks # 67. I got an extra job, which was to clean the approximately twenty offices of the German customs officers. This job was both prestigious and lucrative. Their offices were very luxurious with beautiful desks, and there was so much interesting stuff in each desk. For example, behind one desk was a tin of *speculaas* (Dutch cookies); in the drawer of another was a sausage. Every day I took about 10 *speculaas* cookies from the jar and hid them in the big pockets of my overalls. I took so much from that room to help others. Because my main job was still in the sewing room, I had the brilliant idea of sewing into my overalls a couple of loose bags hanging from my neck with strings. Anything I could take went, *hooops*, into my bag. The largest bag was hanging on top of my thigh. I took *speculaas* that I could trade for food coupons, but the most important items undoubtedly were the cigarette ends. I was very naughty, believe me. I stole so much.

I started an hour earlier than everyone else, before the officers arrived for work. As I left the offices, the Jewish men from the main kitchen rushed over to me to get the cigarette ends. How disgusting to smoke cigarette ends that had been smoked by Nazis. I traded ten cigarette ends for one piece of bread or a milk or cheese coupon. So I did very well: At the camp, they called this "organizing", and I became very popular. Those men let me into the kitchen once, where I saw a very large pot of sauerkraut—the pot was higher than I was. But I jumped up and stuffed two handfuls of sauerkraut into each of my special bags, which I could trade for other food.

I knew that there were no trains taking people to the concentration camps, so what could the Nazis do to me? Only punish me. But that never happened. We were fed a lot of kohlrabi and potatoes and sometimes meat. I provided food for five people: There was an old couple; Aunt Betsie (a niece of my Aunt Marie); and Elte Levi, who was a very large man and a very kosher person and his wife from Dieren. After the war, they all thanked me and later, when I visited Elte Levi in Dieren, he was nice enough to tell me that I had saved his life. He was such a big man that he needed a lot of food. It was good of him to say that, although I doubt that it was really true. But it was true that I was short and didn't need so much food. I always gave away all the extra food. I was able to do a lot of good there.

In Camp Westerbork, I developed a lot of good relationships

Jochebed Katan

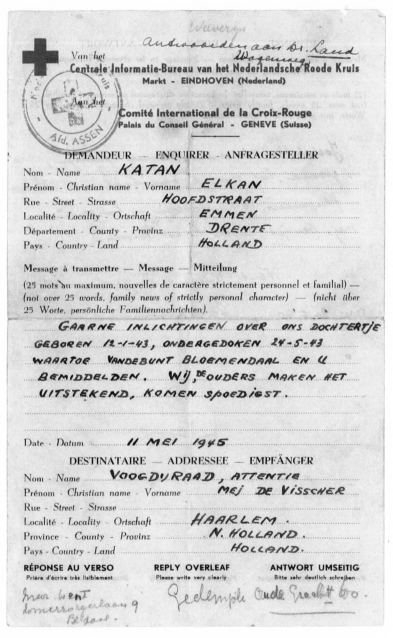

Front (above): May 11, 1945 - Red Cross form used by Elkan to find out about their daughter. Back (next page): May 20, 1945. Papa Went answered: "Jochebed, hiding name Anneke Vanduyn, is healthy, sweet, cheerful, musical. Foster parents, 6 foster brothers, nanny Miss Devries, will miss her."

RÉPONSE   REPLY   ANTWORT

Message à renvoyer au demandeur — Message to be returned to enquirer — Mitteilung an den Anfragesteller zurückzusenden.

(25 mots au maximum, nouvelles de caractère strictement personnel et familial) — (not over 25 words, family news of strictly personal character) (nicht über 25 Worte, nur persönliche Familiennachrichten).

Jochebeth, Schuilnaam: Anneke Vanduyn, is gezond, lief, vroolijk, muzikaal.

Pleegouders, 6 pleegbroertjes en huisgenoote mej. DeVries, Zullen haar missen.

Went, Willems de Zwijgerlaan 108 Overveen.

Date: **20.5 '45**
Datum:

and met old neighbours who knew my parents. I met two men from Czechoslovakia who had a little shoemaker's shop in a shed where they made all kinds of things for the Germans. To my surprise, on the wall, there was an advertising poster from my family's business: van Daelen and van Wessel. It advertised the shoe cream, "DeeWee," that the business sold (the name came from an abbreviation of Daelen and Wessel). The Czechs told me that they had been good customers of my father and had always liked him. They had used the "DeeWee" shoe cream in their leather-tanning and shoe-making business in Brabant, in the south of Holland.

I also met Mr. Van Witsen (of the bookshop), who had been my parents' neighbour in Rotterdam. He was one of the Jewish police. I sneaked over to his barracks in the evenings to visit him because he made me feel comfortable and good. I brought him treats like the *speculaas* cookies, and we played bridge in his little hut. We all needed one another's support to keep up our spirits each day in that depressing place.

Then came the day when the Allies started to fly over the camp. When the guards heard that the Polish and Canadian army was coming our way, they locked all the large barracks so that the Allied soldiers couldn't invade our barracks. I went to the Jewish leader of the camp and told him that most of us thought it was important that all the doors and windows should be kept unlocked. I pointed out that if the Allies decided to bomb the camp, we didn't want to be locked into the barracks. He got the point.

Then the Germans left. We didn't understand why, and we were very wary of the situation. We stayed in the barracks: It seemed the safest place to be. The next day, a Canadian officer arrived at the Camp and made the following announcement: "The camp will be liberated very soon, but, in the meantime, no one is allowed to leave because the Canadian and Polish armies need to have the right of way. The war continues and those armies are working their way up to the north. You all stay here."

Author's Note: *On April 12, 1945, several units of the 2nd Canadian Infantry Division, who were fighting their way north, arrived at Camp Westerbork. The allied military authorities and then the Dutch civilian authorities began the long task of processing the former prisoners. They issued documents and ration books, provided money, and generally smoothed the slow transition back to civilian life. The last of the inmates were not released until the end of June, and within a few weeks, Westerbork was converted into a holding camp for members of the NSB.*

PART 3

CHAPTER 14

Freedom

I had already spoken to four friends in the camp, and we had always said that we would leave as soon as we could, forbidden or not. I had a full suitcase that was too heavy to carry because it was loaded with all the stuff I had stolen. Remember that I had come to the camp with basically nothing. So I went to the two Czech men, who were machinists, and asked them for one or two wheels for my suitcase. I told them that I trusted them and that I was leaving. However, they said they couldn't make the wheels. So we hugged each other good-bye, and this was emotional for me because of our bond through the DeeWee shoe cream poster. I was so touched that they had thought that poster important enough to bring to the camp: It was my last memento of my parents.

On April 12th, 1945, five of us—three men and two women— left the camp. I couldn't carry my suitcase, and I didn't have a wheel for it. The others didn't say, "Well, leave it then." Instead, they grabbed the other end and helped me carry it. We went to #5 Block, cut the barbed wire and crawled out until we came to a very long road, where we were stopped by a huge Polish tank. The Poles spoke French, but it was a dialect we could not understand. We told them in our version of French that we were the Jews from the camp. The Poles allowed us to walk on the edge of the road. There were so many tanks on that road, and they were so close to one another that they almost touched. Finally we arrived at a farm. The farmer's wife welcomed us warmly telling us that we were not the first "of our kind" to come to them.

She let us sleep in the haystack. I was a city girl and had never slept in a haystack before. I never knew that hay makes so much noise—crickets, mice—I could not sleep, but I felt that here was the beginning of FREEDOM. We were so relaxed, and the next morning the wife cooked pancakes on a big open stove—those pancakes were so large and thick. I had never eaten such delicious food in my life. She came with coffee, eggs, and homemade bread. When we were very, very full, we thanked her so much, not knowing how we could ever repay her: We all had tears in our eyes. She is another in the chain of people who welcomed us and who helped to keep alive our faith in the basic goodness of our fellow Dutch people.

We started walking, carrying my heavy suitcase, until we came to a sign that said "Westerbork Village." On the road were five armed Dutch men who would not let us pass. We told them that we had come from the camp and were going back to our families. We still had on the Jewish stars. But no, they would not let us by. But we had luck—a farmer with a very big horse and an empty wagon passed and said, "What! The Jews from the camp! Just put them in my wagon." He promised that he would take us on our way. But first, he wanted to pass the school because they were holding a Dutch man prisoner there; he was a Nazi. Our farmer had stolen his horse and wagon, and he wanted to show this man how the good Dutch people treat the Jews. He drove around the school twice and asked us to please wave to the Dutch Nazi and let him know that now we were free. Then he took us to the next village 10 km away. He was, as he said, a good Dutch man.

Three of our group went their own way, but two of us stayed

together. I took out a shirt from my suitcase, and waved down another wagon. This wagon brought us further towards the village where the van Seijens lived. I was hoping my husband might be hiding somewhere near the village. I was the only one who had any knowledge of the area. It was not so far—only about twenty kilometers or so. Eventually I was on my own. I knocked on the door of a farmhouse and told the farmer that I had to go to Emmer-Compascuum, to the Van Seijen family. He knew the family and lent me a bike, which he would pick up later, and gave me one pound of butter. It took me only one more hour to bike to the van Seijen's with my suitcase on my back.

I arrived at the Van Seijens', and I was so shocked: Bep was eight or nine months pregnant. With tears in her eyes, she told me that her husband had not returned: in fact, none of the five men rounded up after we were betrayed had returned. No one knew where they were. But I knew that when they were in Assen they had been beaten a great deal—the Nazis always beat people around their knees. Someone told me once that if they hit your knees long enough you don't feel it anymore. I knew they had been beaten very badly, and they had not returned. It was an awful feeling: I was free, but they were not. What could I do? The butter was very welcome, for there were three children to feed, with no husband. (Corrie, their daughter, told me later that she remembered my arrival at the house. She says that I was wearing white, leather, heeled shoes that had bands over the feet, a dark blue dress, and a belt that I had made myself out of different colours of electrical wires in Westerbork. She thought it was beautiful.)

And then it happened. Someone came running into the house and said to me, "I just saw your husband walking in Emmen. He looks terrible." Elkan was alive, too! What a joyous reunion it was for Elkan and me. Later, we told each other our stories. He had left the Schuitema's house the day after I was captured; he knew it would be too dangerous to stay. He wandered through the fields in the middle of winter: It was very cold, he had no food, and he did not know where to go. Finally he knocked on a farmhouse door. Once again, a family was willing to help a Jew, even though Elkan was a hunted man. They took him to a house that had a trapdoor to a cellar. Two other men were hiding there as well. In the cellar, there was a linseed oil press and a lot of weapons because they were members of the Underground. Elkan had a very difficult time in the cellar: One of the men was gay, and every night Elkan or the other man had to fight him to get him off his body. After a while, Elkan told the couple upstairs that he couldn't deal with this anymore or he would go insane. Everyone agreed that the gay man would have to go: They found another place for him. That was just before the liberation in April 1945.

Elkan was so thin and in such bad shape. I was in good shape with my well-fed body, and I was much stronger. We realized that we really couldn't stay with at the van Seijens. The five men had not returned, and Bep was very pregnant. Another couple, a mixed Jewish couple, allowed us to stay at their house until the war was really over and we could go back to the west. Every time we needed help, there was someone to help us.

Four days later, on April 20th, I heard, thank God, that all five men had returned. They were full of lice and had been given hardly any food. We heard with horror how they had been punished for their kindness to us. Jan van Seijen was severely beaten in Assen for information. Both Wessel Schuitema and Jan were taken to the Dutch punishment camp in Wilhelmshaven in northern Germany, where they were held from the end of January to the end of the war in April 1945, just after the liberation of Holland. They were hardly given any food, so when Jan returned home, his health was very poor. In 1965, we heard that he had passed away at only 57.

Jan van Seijen showed me the record that he wrote of his arrest, dated June 18, 1945, for the Court in Assen after the war. I noticed how he named all the Dutch men who had collaborated with the

Nazis, providing evidence of just how brutal the Dutch NSB was.

I, undersigned, Jan van Seijen, living in Runde ZZ 32 in Emmer-Compascuum, hereby declare:

On January 2nd, 1945, at about 20:15, the doorbell of my house rang. When I opened the door, I saw about ten men in militia uniforms: Some of them had pistols, others had flashlights shining into my face. The well-known Group Commander, Smit, at that time living in Emmen, stepped forward and commanded "Hands up!" and started to search me. Another Marechaussee [military policeman], W. Platje, stationed in Emmer-Compascuum, told me that the others were going to search my home.

Without my permission, about eight of the militia entered my house, except the aforementioned militiaman [W. Platje]. The previously mentioned Smit, accompanied by W. Bosma van Roswinkel and A. ten Berge van Nieuw-Dordecht, searched my home. The others were unknown to me.

While six were searching the house, Smit asked me rudely, "Have you had guests in the house sometimes?"

Without my permission, he took a framed photo of the royal family off my wall, placed it in his pocket, and did not give it back. This individual ordered me to tell him how I got that picture; I answered that it came in my mail [instead of telling the truth], and then he shouted at me that I was a liar.

In the meantime, the house-search was completed, and they had found my radio. Smit ordered one of the militiamen to take it with them, without my permission, of course. This radio was never given back.

Smit and Bosma ordered me to get dressed, take my bicycle, and go with them. I was brought to the Marechaussee-kazerne [military police base] in Emmer-Compascuum by two militiamen, one of whom was A. ten Berge van Nieuw-Dordecht. I was locked up under the orders of those two until the afternoon of January 3rd. My bicycle was never given back to me.

On January 3rd, four militiamen whom I did not know

brought me to the militia building in Emmen, and I was interviewed by General Smit, W. Bosma, and a third person, whose name is probably Warring or Warrink. It was a short interview where they tried to have me declare that I had given shelter to Jews. After that, I was brought to the police station in Emmen and imprisoned there.

On January 4th, at about 20:00, I was brought back to one of the rooms in the militia building. Inside were Smit and Bosma, another militiaman in uniform, three people in black-and-green uniforms, and one civilian. These five others were unknown to me. Behind the desk sat a girl, about twenty years old, named Alfering or Alferink.

When I came in, Bosma ordered me to take my overcoat off. I was immediately beaten by Bosma and three or four of the other unknown men in uniform, with rubber truncheons, metal bars, and bare fists. This went on for fifteen minutes. I was beaten on my face, back, shoulders, in fact, everywhere they could hit me. During that time, the civilian, Smit, and the girl were playing the role of interested witnesses.

After this beating, I was told "that I had granted lodging to Jews, and I had better confess it." With all kinds of questions, remarks, abusive comments and insults, sometimes coming out of two, three, or more mouths at the same time, they tried to make me confess to helping and sheltering the Jews. The "gentlemen" were cursing heavily and the girl watched the entire time, while Smit was generally the one who spoke. Sometimes the civilian asked me some questions and made some notes.

After my denial, the same people mistreated me again, twice, each time for approximately fifteen minutes and in the same way as before. When I kept denying the charge, they brought in Mrs. Katan, who came from Amsterdam, who had hidden in my house for several months in 1944, and [my neighbour] W. Schuitema, who lived in Emmer-Compascuum. One after the other, the two declared that she [Katan] had been with me, and that I had brought her to him, Schuitema. When I, despite those declarations, kept denying this, Bosma threatened, "I will have you carried out of this room as a dead body." When he said that, Smit nodded in agreement. Then they asked me if I had received ration coupons for Jews, and from whom. They told me that the S.D. [Sickerheitsdienst – the SS intelligence agency] would find out for them.

On Sunday, January 7, at about 7:00, Bosma and another militiaman, who said his name was Oost, brought me to the land militia in Assen. After one week in that police station, and then ten days in the Assen prison, where I was locked up, I was brought to a detention camp in Germany. On April 20, 1945 I returned to Emmer-Compascuum.

This is truthfully written.
Emmer-Compascuum, June 18, 1945.

Later I found out that Mr. Pepping was a member of the Resistance. He knew that the Dutch Nazi *Landwachters* were coming, so he had already fled to his mother's house in Assen. Why did he not warn the other men? Maybe he had no time. He was not exactly a gentleman, and kept raising the price for our food. But he had saved our lives.

CHAPTER 15

Finding Jeantje (Jochebed)

We left the van Seijens and went to Emmen, a small town in the east of Holland. The mayor of the town started an organization to sort out all the stuff that had been stored in a vacant factory. The Germans had stolen so much from the Dutch, including the Dutch Jews, but it was now to be redistributed to the starving people. Elkan was asked to organize its shipment to those in the west who needed it so badly. He was glad of the work, for he was unemployed. He was the main organizer, with about eight volunteers to help him. There were four Dutch army trucks, and every week a convoy went to the west full and came back empty.

Elkan became good friends with John, one of the Dutch military drivers, and said to him, "Listen, John, every week I give you full trucks to go to the west and you come back with empty trucks. But please next time come back with a 'full truck' for me—find my daughter." John replied, "Well, you are in luck. I am driving to North Holland next Thursday. I will check with the International Red Cross to find your daughter's address."

And so, in June 1945, John did indeed come back with "a full truck." All bridges in the country had been destroyed, and it took a while for him to get to the Amsterdam area and return to Emmen. We waited in suspense for a long time. He gave us the news that he had found Jeantje's name in the lists and learned that she was alive. He had the address of her hiding place, in the town of Bloemendaal near Amsterdam. John visited Mr. van de Bunt there, and he was given a little photo of Jeantje to bring to us. I am still emotional when I think about his return with that photo. I can hardly talk about it—it was so moving. We did not sleep that night. When Mr. van Seijen heard the news about Jeantje, he made a little wooden car for her. We owe a special thank you to Jan and Bep Van Seijen and their family. What those people have meant to us. The feelings Jan and Bep had for us were so exceptional, so compassionate. We felt so supported.

We had to leave, but that was not so easy—until someone came by with an old car that he had kept through the war. It was an old Citroën, with room for lots of passengers. We bought the car from him with the last of our money. We put two people on the bumper, three on top of the front, one outside on the trunk, three in the front seats, and three in the back—twelve in total in the car—and we said good-bye to the good couple where Elkan spent the last weeks. They gave Elkan six bottles of corn oil to take for the *ouders* (war parents) of our child. How sweet; I still feel moved by that. That was so exceptional—they were such good people—like so many others who risked their own lives to help others, including the Jews.

All twelve people climbed into/onto the car. It was almost riding on its two back wheels and the axel nearly broke when the car hit a pothole. It is hard to believe that we arrived in the west. I can't remember the route we took because so many bridges were destroyed. I remember driving past Arnhem—the city was totally destroyed. Finally Elkan and I arrived in Bloemendaal; by that time we were the only two left in the car.

We drove down the Went family's street (*Zomerzorgerlaan*)

and suddenly I squeezed Elkan's arm and said, "Look. There she is! Standing there." He said, "Stay calm now. Suppose that is not her." But she looked just like my twin sister. "I am an identical twin. I can see my sister in her. It must be Jeantje."

Dik Went, the second-youngest Went brother, later told me he remembers very well the day that we came to pick up our little girl. He could tell that we felt strange and out of place, not knowing how to deal with the situation. We all stood in the front garden of the Willem de Zwijgerlaan home.

The Wents were such a marvelous family. Mr. Went was a director/owner of a big insurance firm. There were six boys, all two years apart. The entire family was so happy to see us. Papa Went was sitting at the table and you could tell that he loved his little girl. They had renamed her Anneke to keep her safe from the Nazis. He loved his six boys, but that little Anneke … he loved her so dearly. And Papa Went had always said that in case the parents did not return, he would take care that she would be placed in a good Jewish family. "She is Jewish and she belongs there." All respect to him, as he idolized her.

The boys had a box with toys and coloured pencils, and there were some bikes, although not in good condition. The Germans had confiscated all rubber, including the rubber tires, so the boys rode their bikes on the bare rims. In two weeks, they were thoroughly broken.

That night we were allowed to sleep in Peter's room with the baby bed, and that night I took Jeantje out of the bed four times to let her pee or just to hold her. As my twin sister and I were the youngest in the family, there had been no younger children in the house.

The Wents welcomed us into their home for two weeks while we were getting to know Jeantje. We were strangers to her, and we too felt strange. I wasn't used to children at all. When I was at the Van Seijens, I did ask Bep to sing some children's songs, so I could write them down. So I was prepared in a way. But thank God, it all worked out. Peter told me later that he remembered Anneke cried when she had to leave with us. Naturally, it would take a while before she accustomed herself to her new parents.

CHAPTER 16

Our Little Girl's Story

Now, at last, we found out how our little daughter had fared while we were in hiding. When Mrs. van de Bunt had carried Jeantje away that terrible day, she knew that she could not keep her in Amsterdam, as it was far too dangerous. She brought her to the Went family. They lived in a little village called Bloemendaal, which was close to Amsterdam. The Wents had six boys between the ages of five and thirteen, and a beloved female German shepherd named Ducky. Joep was the oldest boy; Daan was second; Flip was born on Oct. 15, 1933; Peter, born Jan. 12, 1935; Dik, born May 5, 1936; Aat, born Oct. 22, 1938. Our little girl became the baby of their family.

They had a live-in nanny, Martha, who was about twenty-five years old. She loved the baby dearly and kept a diary for me, which she kept hidden. She made the cover from a piece of thin cardboard and illustrated it herself with paint. She pasted in baby pictures and even glued in a little piece of her hair. She describes the baby's arrival into the Went family:

It is the 24th of May of the year 1943 when a small woolen parcel is carried by a lady into the Went family home. Wrapped in that parcel is a very lovely little girl who is 4 months old. Her little bright eyes beam happily into the world. When Mrs. Went takes her over from the lady, a smile passes over the little girl's face. Fortunately she knows nothing yet of the miserable situation that forced her parents to give up their little baby for the time being.

Poor parents. How are they feeling at this moment, robbed of their freedom? Chased and scared like animals, they are trying to find a hiding place that is safe from the German murderers. When Mrs. Went lowers the baby into the cradle, the baby cries for a moment. What else could she expect? Might not her own mother have cuddled her a little too much in the last few days?

At 10 o'clock that night, she gets her last bottle. Half asleep, she empties it, then drops her tiny head back onto the pillow. The little rose-coloured thumb is searching for its familiar place. Mrs. Went softly touches the little head: "'Jochebed,' as your name is no longer permitted, so we will call you 'Julie'—'Julie van de Zomer' because we live on Zomerzorgerlaan, and with 'Julie,' your first initial will remain the same."

Now it is quiet again in the room. Three children breathing: Little Adrian (Aad), Little Dikkie, and the new little sister. Darkness and stillness. The day is over. An important day in your life that you will not remember later.

The Wents recalled the baby's arrival. Papa and Mama Went told the boys that her parents had died in the German bombardment of Rotterdam, which had been back in 1940, so would not have been true. However, the boys were young, and they accepted the story without question. They were told not to tell anyone about the arrival of the new baby, but Dik was so excited that the next day in school he promptly told everyone in his class that he had the loveliest baby girl in the world in the house. The teachers

l-r: Martha, Anneke, Aadje, Dikkie, Peter, Flip, Daan and Joep Went

must have known better than to believe that her parents had died in the Rotterdam bombardment, but nothing was said. Far more dangerous was the fact that little Aad told people around the village that he had a Jewish sister. Thankfully he was so young that no one believed him, but it was a wonder that he knew his new sister was Jewish at all; maybe he had been listening at the door of his parents' room. I still wonder about the people in the village; some of them must have guessed that the Wents were looking after a Jewish baby. Yet everyone seems to have kept the secret: This was special.

Since the boys had such a hard time keeping secrets, the Wents decided to change her name to Anneke van Duin. The boys loved the name Anneke because there is a little rhyme in Dutch called Anneke Tanneke Toverheks (Magic Witch), and they had a lot of fun with that. She was put into the same bedroom as the two youngest brothers, Aad and Dikkie. The boys loved her very much. She was their baby sister, and they played with her and taught her to speak and to walk. "Papa Went," as Anneke called him, was especially charmed to have a little girl to whom he could give nice skirts and all kinds of girlish things.

It was wonderful for me to read the entries in Martha's diary, telling me so many details about our little girl's life with the Wents:

Aunt Martha's Baby Book. May 1943 - May 1945.
Martha made this 40-page book in case Anneke's parents came back for her. She wanted them (and Anneke!) to have a permanent memory of the wonderful time she spent with the Went family.

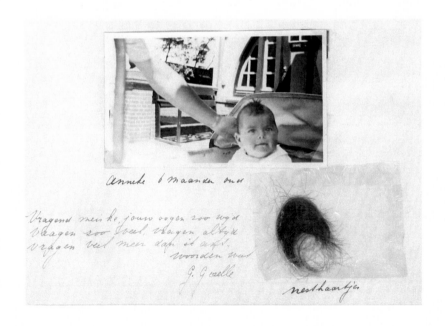

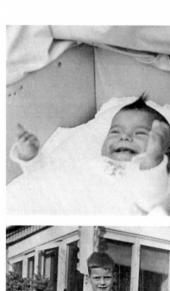

Some of the many photos contained in Annke's Baby Book including this one of Anneke with Aad Went walking in the 'forest'.

Martha with Anneke and Mama Went.

1944 - Anneke on Papa Went's knee.

1944 - Anneke with Martha.

Anneke grows like a cabbage—tanned by the sun and healthy. When the weather is good, she spends the entire day in the garden. The boys are crazy about their sister; especially for Peter, she is a miracle. Often he creeps up to her to have a little chat. Anneke cries out happily. She pulls his hair when he bows his head to kiss her. Peter loves it and so does Anneke. When you have five brothers, it is very special to suddenly get a little sister.

"Later," says Peter, "I am going to marry her."

The others laugh about this, but for him it was dead serious.

Three weeks after that first May Day, suddenly Julie van de Zomer needs to be changed to Anneke van Duin. The police are looking for her. Happily, it turns out well, and nobody uses the name Julie anymore. She is now Anneke, and the boys say "Anneke Tanneke Toverheks".

A child's first discoveries are the most exciting. We can no longer remember what it is like to see things for the first time. But she was a little child in her first year of life seeing the world for the first time. Anneke peers at the thick elephant in her playpen, which her mother had made for her. She has a little stick and she repeatedly pokes it into the empty spool of thread. Her lips are pursed in concentration. Suddenly a sunbeam shines into the playpen and she tries to grasp it 10 or 20 times. She laughs and laughs.

Then she grabs the bars of the playpen, stretches, reaches up, and voila, Anneke is standing. She is so proud of herself. Mother Went sees Anneke standing and lifts the laughing child high in the air. "Anneke, how you have grown. On the 7th of October you can stand. We will remember this very well, because, if your mother comes back, she has to know everything about you as a baby." Then she put Anneke back into the playpen, but after two minutes, Anneke stands up again. She is radiant. Her legs want to stamp with the joy of it. Up and down her body is dancing, and the dance is exciting on its own. She can stand—her joy is contagious. A step in the journey to adulthood.

December 5th, 1943:
Sint Nicolaas is a wonderful celebration, especially when you get a lot of presents. But if you are still lying in a crib, you are not that interested; not interested in the rhymes that the adults compose for you either. But it is pleasant if the adults keep them for you, so that later, you may read them for yourself. I didn't keep the rest of the presents, because by the time you read this, those little clothes will not fit you anyway, and I think the baby rattle will be broken by then.

12 January 1944:
Anneke celebrates her first birthday. Coincidentally, her brother and best friend, Peter, has the same birthday. She is dressed in her most beautiful dress, and Peter in his Sunday suit. That is traditional on your birthday. Both the chairs are decorated. After the traditional song, "Happy Birthday," Peter enters the room with Anneke in his arms. "Hip, hip, hooray." Anneke gazes around with her big eyes, and doesn't understand what is happening.
Now it is presents time. They open their presents in turn. Anneke can't open her presents herself yet, but the others loved to do that for her. She loves it all, but doesn't really understand it. Next, she is put into her decorated chair for her porridge. Everyone enjoys the baby. That day, she was often taken out of the playpen and showed off to the aunts and friends. Anneke is happy sitting on their laps.
That evening after dinner, as it happens at every birthday, comes the big moment. The lights are dimmed, and a delicious cake with nine candles is brought in. And this time, it is followed by a little cake with one candle. Anneke is on Father Went's lap and enjoys the flames. Now it is bedtime. Good night all. May you celebrate many birthdays, little pussycat, and may you always stay so sweet, so you will always give your parents a lot of pleasure. Looking at you sleeping, I think of the face of your mother, which I have never seen.

The Wents were threatened by the Germans. After the war, Peter Went told Jochebed the story about Papa Went's summons. In 1944, the Germans ordered that all non-Jewish Dutch men between 16 and 40 were to go to Silesia to work in factories for the war "effort." One day, two young blond NSB men came to the house in the Willem de Zwijgerlaan at dinnertime. The entire family, six sons, one daughter (Anneke), Mama and Papa Went and Nanny Martha were all sitting around the table. The NSB men had come to collect Papa Went for factory work as he fell into the age band. Papa Went looked in the eyes of the youngest man, about 24 years old, and asked the man if he had any children. He had a young daughter. Papa Went told the young man that he was the only breadwinner and that he could not leave because his family, sitting here, would die. How could the young man force him to abandon that responsibility? The two men bowed their heads and left. Little did they know that there was someone else in that house as well, hiding in the garage—an English pilot. But little Anneke's world remained stable:

The months pass quickly, and spring is around the corner. Anneke plays in the sandbox; fortunately, she cannot climb out. Then the summer arrives, and when it is very warm weather, she wears a bright red swimming suit and plays in a metal basin full of water. She enjoys that and laughs from joy and pleasure. When Dikkie makes funny faces at her, she copies them exactly. She has a very strong will. If she doesn't want to do something, she will not do it. If we try to let her walk, she pulls her knees up. She is crawling and we must be content with that: She does not want to walk. She crawls through the entire house, even up the stairs. She crawls around all summer, until Papa Went puts her in the middle of the room, sits himself in a chair and says, "Now, you have to walk to me." She looks at him and sees from his face that he is serious: And then, she begins to walk to him. It is wobbly, but it is so sweet. After a week, she walks very well, and after a month, she is chasing the boys on their way to school.

In September 1944, the Germans evicted the Went family from their home, and they had to move to Overveen, Willem de Zwijgerlaan. As there was such a shortage of vehicles, they used anything they could to move their belongings. They even used a toy baker's cart owned by the boys. In the diary, Martha wrote Anneke's reaction to the move:

> *September 1944:*
> *Then September comes and we have to evacuate. We are happy to get an entire house for the family because most people have to share houses with other families. We are going from Bloemendaal to Overveen, Willem de Zwijgerlaan. Anneke shouts with every piece of furniture that is carried out of the house. She liked the neatness and now suddenly everything is being moved around: She doesn't like that at all. Fortunately, there is a friendly lady who takes her to her house. Anneke stays there for a week. When she is brought into the new house, she stands and looks around bemusedly. Happily, she discovers her own chair, and that evening, finds her bear in her bed. Of course, after a week she is totally used to it and knows exactly where the cookies are. That was the most important thing for her.*

The new house was an old school building, so all the bedrooms had numbers on the doors. Peter remembers that it was by a dirty canal, but the canal has since been cemented over and is currently a road. However, Flip remembers it differently and says that it was not a canal but a German built trench that was used as a barrier to divert enemy tanks. The walls of the trench were lined with trees and there was a track in the centre that carried the cut trees along the trench. The Went boys would take rides on the cart for fun and would sometimes steal trees to bring home for firewood.

For the boys, the danger of Anneke's discovery really was constant. Sometimes, without realizing it, they could bring undesired attention to Anneke. The timber pole incident is one example. Everyone was in search of firewood, and the Wents' neighbours in Overveen were stealing timber poles from the Germans who had erected them in the small meadow of an NSB neighbour's backyard so that Allied pilots parachuting down from their destroyed planes could not land there. The boys had a special code name for the NSB-ers: They called them "Noten Sinaasappelen Bananen" (nuts oranges bananas).

Flip and Dik decided that they too would steal poles to provide their family with firewood. Peter did the stealing, while Dik distracted the NSB-er in the guardhouse at the corner of the street. It was Daan's job to cut them up into firewood. This had been working very well, until one day, everything went wrong. Dik was unable to distract the NSB-er just as Peter unaccountably ran straight home with the pole, instead of heading down the lane.

The result was that the NSB-ers came to the Went house. At that time, not only were the Wents hiding Anneke, but they also had an English pilot hiding in the garage. They often gave shelter to pilots who had been shot down by the Germans. As well, in the garage, the Wents kept a "crystal" radio set, which was highly illegal, to listen to BBC newscasts. The guards found nothing.

The Hunger Winter of 1944-45 meant to me that the trains no longer ran from Camp Westerbork to the east. But to the Dutch people in the three western cities of Rotterdam, Amsterdam, and The Hague, the winter of 1945 was the time that the railway workers went on strike, and there was no shipment of food or coal by rail or canal to their cities. Everyone was hungry and cold and many people starved to death. Many ate the tulip bulbs for food.

Author's Note: *In September 1944, the national railway strike and Seyss-Inquart's cancellation of all barges and ships crippled the movement of food and supplies to the west of Holland. In October, most gas and electrical systems failed, leaving everyone reliant on coal or wood for fuel. By mid-*

December, the daily rations in the cities had declined to 630 calories per person. People were eating anything they could get, including tulip bulbs. Over the course of that cold winter, more than 20,000 Dutch civilians died of starvation. By April 9, malnutrition was responsible for 54 percent of all fatalities. Finally, on April 28th, the Swedish Air Force began the process of dropping hundreds of thousands of rations of white bread over western Holland. "Operation Manna" continued daily through to May 8. This ended the terrible Hunger Winter

Martha talks in her diary about the hardness of the Hunger Winter:

The winter of 1944-45:
A terrible winter for many, many people. Hunger and cold. Small children with bare feet call at the door and beg for a slice of bread. As we are making many bicycle trips to the farms in the north of Holland, we still have enough to eat. Anneke is hardly aware of our toil and moil. She only notices that at least once a week somebody disappears and is cheered back home the next day. She stretches her arms to join the party, too. The bicycle bags are opened and when the milk bottles appear, Anneke quickly toddles to the fore with her drinking cup. If only the provider of this priceless liquid could see the joy it brings to the children.

Joep, the eldest brother, or Flip used to ride their bicycles to the farmlands in the north, taking a shortcut across the IJsselmeer. Each week, they traded bed linens from home for milk and food. But the whole family decided that it was Ducky, the dog, who took the best care of the family during the Hunger winter. Ducky snatched the neighbour's pet rabbit and dashed back with it to his house. By the time the neighbours realized their rabbit was missing, the Went family had already eaten it. The boys nearly starved that winter.

Finally, in May, the war ended, and food began to flow into Holland. The Red Cross sent three of the Went boys to other countries, so they could recuperate: Daan was sent to Scotland, and Aad and Dik were sent to different cities in Switzerland. Peter said he never felt hungry because, like many of the Dutch, he ate the tulip bulbs. He told me they didn't taste too bad. Martha records the end of the war in her diary, and describes the family's reaction when Mr. Went tells the boys Anneke's real story:

> *The end of the war:*
> *Then finally comes that eventful day, May 4th, 1945. At nine in the evening, the radio announces that the German forces have withdrawn from the Netherlands. By half-past nine the streets are filled with cheering and dancing people: Long live the Queen! The next morning the red, white, and blue flag of Holland is flown from every house: Holland is free again. Eight o'clock the next morning is the moment of the official surrender. We sing several songs at the piano.*
> *Then Mr. Went, Anneke's beloved foster father, tells his sons Anneke's story. He tells them, "Anneke will soon be leaving." Anneke listens with eyes wide open. The boys are very upset that she is leaving. "But you will visit us often, won't you?" they ask. Anneke is naughty and says, "No." She realizes that she is supposed to say, "Yes." She has all the fun in the world.*
> *Full of anxiety, we are waiting for a message regarding Anneke's parents. Luckily, there soon arrives a letter from the Red Cross: "Enquiries regarding our daughter. Her parents are doing extremely well."*
> *Oh Anneke, your Daddy and Mama are still alive, and they are coming soon to pick you up. Look! That letter is for you. Anneke appreciates the little red cross the most. She touches it all the time.*
> *"We are coming soon."*
> *What a joy for parents to reunite with their sweet little girl.*

Years later, the Went boys told Jochebed about liberation day. Peter remembered the Canadian soldiers who handed out white bread and jam in the town. He also remembered being taken to the hospital that day. He had climbed onto a tank and snagged his leg on a shovel lying on the tank. He is proud of that scar, and to him the V shape means: "V for Victory." Aad remembers the Canadian soldiers sleeping in the courtyard of his school. The Canadians gave all the boys delicious food from their mess tins.

Martha's diary even records the day we came to find "Anneke." It is a heart-warming record kept by a wonderful woman. We treasure this diary.

The second big day in Anneke's life:
And then comes the day. This one she won't be able to remember either. It is late Tuesday afternoon, a quarter to six. Anneke is playing outside with the boys. She is wearing a blue coat and a dark blue ribbon in her hair. This is how Ankeke's parents see their child as their car moves through the gate onto the driveway.
They immediately say, "There she is!"
Of course, Anneke is a little shy at first. But that very same evening, the real Mama gets many kisses. She is still a little afraid of Papa. The Mama wears glasses, and Anneke finds that quite special. As a treat, she is allowed to sleep with her parents in the same room. This is an even greater joy for the parents than for Anneke. I guess the parents did not get much sleep because of sheer happiness.

Summer 1945, Overveen:
Dearest Anneke,
Now you are neither Anneke van Duin nor Julie van de Zomer anymore. You have your own name back: Jochebed Katan. This name you will keep always from now on.
You came as a small chubby baby to us. Now you are a real girl with a pleased little face when you wore the new dress that

your Mother knitted for you. You will have lots of pleasures in your life, as I can tell from your twinkling eyes.

Later when you are older, you will not remember these first years of your life. That's why I made this album for you. Cherish it and never forget what your foster parents have done for you. They have loved you as if you were their own child. You were the little princess with all these boys. Six brothers you have had, who loved you so dearly: Aat, Dittie, Pépé, Pip, Daan and Poepie. They have played so much with you.

I hope that you will some day have a brother or a sister and that you will be as sweet for them as the Wents have been for you.

You are musical, because when you were one-and-a-half years old, you already knew lots of tunes and when Daan played the piano you always wanted to sit on his lap. Sing of the sun and the spring for yourself and others.

We wish you nothing but happiness and wellbeing! Bye, bye, dear little Anneke. Thanks for the sunlight you have brought us in these difficult war years.

Martha

Lieve Jeantje, Papa's kleuter
Mama's groote stoute snoes
Kwikje's veel geplaagde plaaggeest
(Papa Went, die noemt je poes!)

En de groote Wenten-jongens
Zeggen : Anneke Katan
Martha, die zegt : schatteboutje,
Hoeveel namen heb je dan?

Gaf ik je voor elk naampje
Weer een ander nieuw geschenk
Dan zou jou dat wel bevallen
Maar als ik me nu bedenk

Dat er nog zoo heel veel kind'ren
Wachtend zijn op een cadeau
Dan moet ik wel zunig wezen
En doe ik het maar zoo!

Sinterklaas,
5 Dec 1946

Lieve groote Jeantje - poes
Papa Went vindt je een snoes
Mama Went vindt jou een schat
Die haar hart gestolen had.

Jeantje ben je nu al 4 ?
Heb je vandaag veel plezier?
Zal je Beer zijn kleeren strijken?
Zoo dat hij 'net-echt' zal lijken?

Jeantje kom eens gauw logeeren
Dan zal Papa Went probeeren
Of hij nog een poes kan teek'nen
Maar je mag er niet op reek'nen

Lieve poes nu schei ik uit
Stuur je een kus nog tot besluit
Poepie zal de brief je geven
"Lang zal Jeanne poes nog leven!"

Papa Went
12 Jan 1947

Two lovely poems written by Papa Went for Jeantje (the name Jochebed's parents called her from birth) after the war. In the first one, he writes as Santa Claus (Sinterklaas) about all of the different names Jeantje has had. In the second one, he writes about how much the entire family misses her.

CHAPTER 17

Making a New Start

As we had no house to go to, the Went family invited us to stay for two weeks in their house. During that time, Mr. van de Bunt came to visit, and Elkan had a private talk with him, hoping to get his old job back at the office of Starreveld and van de Bunt. But Mr. van de Bunt could not make him that offer as there was not yet enough work to warrant his employment. I remember there were loud, angry voices coming from the study.

However, we were invited to stay with the van de Bunt family in Bloemendaal. They were wonderful people. Mr. van de Bunt was the local director of the Red Cross. Mrs. van de Bunt, his wife, who had picked up my baby, had tried to save other babies as well during the war. She told us about a sad case. On October 16th, 1942, a foundling was laid in front of their door, on de Duinwijckweg 1 in Bloemendaal. It was a baby boy, and he was given the name Remy van Duinwijck. After the war, they learned that his real name was Koenraad Huib Gezang. They took in the baby, but not two weeks later, on October 30th, 1942, the Sicherheitspolizei (Security Police) ordered Mrs. van de Bunt to bring little Remy to their office on de Euterpestraat 99 in Amsterdam and leave him there. The Jewish

Council intervened, and Remy was taken to the daycare opposite the Dutch Theatre on the Plantage Middenlaan in Amsterdam. There was a great effort to keep little Remy out of the hands of the Germans, but this was unsuccessful, and so he was put on a train to Westerbork. Little Remy was deported to the Sobibor camp, where he was killed on the May 21st, 1943 at the age of seven months. The stark realities of this war were that our baby was saved and another was killed. Mrs. van de Bunt tried to save both. All my life I never forgot how lucky we were.

When we stayed with the van de Bunts, they themselves had just had such a terrible tragedy. Their little daughter, Mary, had been killed on April 16, 1943, by a British bomb that fell on their house—a terrible example of friendly fire. They still had their sons, Lisa and Alekka, but can you imagine how tragic the situation was— we were reunited with our little girl, and their little girl had been killed? This was so wrong. They had grief, and we had happiness.

I didn't know what to do with myself when we stayed with them. I was not allowed to do anything in that house because there was a maid, so I had nothing to do. Every morning at 8:00 I went walking with Jeantje. But she needed a lot of sleep, so I had to put her to bed at 10:30 each morning. There was not much electricity. The odd time I was allowed to iron Mr. Van de Bunt's shirt, I quickly ironed Elkan's too, for he only had two shirts.

Every morning, Elkan went to Amsterdam in a car with six others and walked 10-12 hours, a day in search of a house. One day in Amsterdam he was sitting on the edge of the van Hulstplein fountain, absolutely exhausted, when a mailman came to him and asked him kindly why he looked so tired. Elkan told him that he was walking around looking for a house to rent because we had just come out of hiding because of the war.

The mailman was kindness itself. He told him that getting a house was no problem. He knew exactly which apartments were empty. He knew that in Geuzenstraat 25, III, the police were just now evicting two NSB-ers and the house was standing empty. The mailman even knew who had the key and organized everything for us to move in.

So on August 2nd, 1945, we moved in there for a while. Then on January 8th, 1946, we moved again to Stadionweg 213. We had been a very happy and loving couple until the war started, and Jeantje was put in hiding alone and we too were in hiding. Thank God, we found each other again, but then began the very difficult time after the war. We really had nothing. How could I cook on a small potbellied stove? Everyone had already been doing this for two years. Little coals were placed on top, and we had to blow from below. If we wanted potatoes, the cooking time was two hours. For everything, you had to line up.

Once, at the vegetable store, Jeantje put her white stuffed bear down on a gate, and it was stolen. Peter Went had given this bear, his best toy, to her, and her sorrow could not be stopped. The bear was irreplaceable.

Then we moved from Amsterdam into my grandfather's house in Scheveningen. It was on the corner on the Harstenhoek weg, number 97. Scheveningen is a small fishermen's resort close to The Hague. The house was in very bad condition: Everything made of wood had been stripped off and used as fuel in the cold winter of 1944-'45; there were no wooden floors anymore, and most of the staircase steps were gone, as well. The houses just around the corner in de Gentsestraat had been completely levelled in the heavy bombardment. In the beginning, it was very difficult to live there, but we found one room that we could live in. Gradually, we began to rebuild the house and to rebuild our new life. Elkan went back to his job at Mr. van de Bunt's office. Later, he got a job as a registered accountant in The Hague on the Kneuterdijk 7. He worked there for many years until he decided to open his own practice in our house.

9 May 1945 - The headline reads: "Amsterdammers, we are free!"

An historic moment in Amsterdam: A parade for Queen Wilhelmina on June 28, 1945. This photo was taken by an employee of the van de Bunt company.

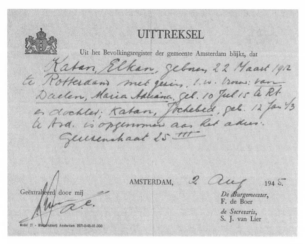

Rie and Elkan's permission to live in their new house in Amsterdam.
August 2nd, 1945.

August 1946 - the wedding of Aunt Martha. Anneke was the flower girl.

CHAPTER 18

The Fate of Elkan's Family

Almost all members of my family were murdered, but remarkably, Elkan's mother and all his four siblings survived the war. Ans, Elkan's oldest sister, and Louis, his older brother, lived in the south of Holland where they managed to escape detection. Eva (Eef), the younger sister, obtained false identity papers and went into hiding in The Hague; her false name was Anna Maria de Groot, and her occupation was listed as housekeeper. Elkan's mother, Judikje Katan-Sanders, who had been widowed for a good many years, went into hiding with Mrs. G. Mulder, Kerkhoflaan 58, Rotterdam. She was only about 1.3 km or 16 min. walking distance from her own house at Noordmolenstraat 66, Rotterdam. She and her son, Richard, exchanged a number of letters during the war. After the war, "Moeder Mulder" (Mother Mulder) was loved and respected and was always the guest of honor at the Katan family gatherings.

Elkan's younger brother, Richard, and his wife, Roosje, decided that they would neither obey the Germans nor go into hiding. Instead, they would live as non-Jews, with false identities. It was to Richard's great advantage that he did not look Jewish.

His business friend, Henk Wientjes, from Dordrecht, stole

identity cards from two workers, who were of similar age to Richard and Roosje, from the locker room of his local V&D department store. Richard and Roosje became Hendrik Simon ('Henk') den Boef and Grietje Barendregt. These two people were unrelated, but Richard doctored the identity cards, slipping in their own pictures over the originals and documenting their marriage. They then removed their yellow badges (Stars of David) with "Jood" stamped on them and left Rotterdam by train on July 29, 1942, carrying only their suitcases. They spent six weeks in a holiday bungalow in Oisterhout and then rented a room with the Leur family in Arnhem.

Like his brother Louis, Richard became involved in the underground resistance movement. His landlord, Jacob Leur, worked at the Arnhem City Hall, where he and another man had access to various blank ID papers and stamps. Richard, in collaboration with these two men, produced papers to keep young men out of slave labour in Germany. He was also involved in other types of resistance work. Eventually, seemingly, his luck ran out. On April 4th, 1944, he and his wife Roosje (who had changed her name from Grietje to Gerrie) were travelling by train from The Hague on resistance business. Between the stations of Gouda and Woerden, Dutch members of the German security police passed through the train, checking passengers' identity cards. Richard carried a new counterfeit identity card, made for him by the resistance group. However, the resistance group that manufactured these identity cards had recently been arrested, and the numbers and characteristics of their counterfeit products were known. Richard was arrested.

He was first brought to the police bureau in Utrecht, then to Scheveningen prison for questioning, and then to the Amersfoort prison camp to await transportation to Germany as slave labour. With remarkable sangfroid, Richard, who spoke German, managed to convince the Germans that he was not involved in illegal activities. He had only been trying to dodge the work procurement by carrying papers with a false birth date. Luck was with him this time because the central record office that held copies of all identity papers in the Netherlands – Kunstzaal Kleykamp –had just been destroyed by the RAF in a precision bombardment on April 11, 1942. That made it impossible for the Germans to discover that Richard was not Henk den Boef, that his papers had been reported stolen, and that not just his birth date but his entire identity was a fake.

Richard was released from Amersfoort camp on July 7, 1944, thanks to the doctor who had to approve prisoners for slave labour in Germany. At the request of the resistance, he told the Germans that Richard had hepatitis and was, thus, useless for labour. Richard sent a telegram to his mother on the morning of his release from the Amersfoort prison camp. He signed that telegram "Richard" instead of "Henk." Luck was with him again—it was never discovered by the authorities.

Richard returned to Arnhem and resumed his resistance activities with a vengeance. His wife later told their son that Richard kept hand grenades on their cellar stairs. Fortunately, on September 17, 1944, the British launched Operation Market Garden and landed a large airborne force near Arnhem in order to capture the Rhine bridge. German administration and control became a shambles. In late April 1945, 'Henk' and 'Gerrie' were liberated by the Canadian forces in Beekbergen. Richard and Roosje resumed their own names and revealed that they were Jews. Their friends could hardly believe it, and some kept calling them Henk and Gerrie for years.

Elkan's Uncle Mozes (Uncle Mau) and family were not so lucky. Mau was a very wealthy man, who had established the first department store in The Hague where people could buy on the installment plan; they could purchase furs, shoes, stoves and many other things. This was modernity in the 1920. People paid their weekly installments to a collector who went from door to door. The department store was so successful that Mau and his wife, Aunt Fie (Sophia Jacoba), moved to a big house along the main canal, The Koninginnegracht in The Hague. Aunt Fie had a chauffeured limousine, and she and her two daughters were very snobbish. The house was filled with beautiful large paintings, Persian tapestries, and an 18th century Amsterdam grandfather clock. She gave parties for charity in their library, where the guests, wearing their modish hats, sat on gilded chairs. The library had wallpaper with French lilies, and the powder room was like a boudoir. Most extraordinary in 1925 in the Netherlands.

They never heeded the Nazi threat. Perhaps they felt that their wealth and their position would protect them. Two years after the Nazis invaded Holland in 1940, they were rounded up by the Germans. Their daughter, Marianne Eva Nitzowitsch-Katan, with her husband and children, tried to enter Switzerland, but they were denied admittance. The Nazis rounded them up in the south of France, and they were killed in Auschwitz on 21 August 1943.

Aunt Fie and Uncle Mau were driven to the train station by their butler. Aunt Fie brought 24 suitcases with her. Uncle Mau said to his butler, who drove them to the station, "Jan, as soon as the war is over, pick me up and, if necessary, charter a plane."

Uncle Mau and Aunt Fie were gassed in Sobibor on 14 May, 1943. They were two of the 94 Katans killed during the war. (Hebrew University of Jerusalem - centre for research on Dutch Jewry. In Memoriam.)

Their son, Emiel, participated in the resistance movement. His job was espionage for the Ordedienst (OD), a group preparing for the return of the exiled Dutch government and the Dutch secret service. On July 11th, 1941 he was caught in The Hague, sent to prisons in Scheveningen and Utrecht, and ultimately deported to Sachsenhausen where he was shot May 3rd, 1942. He was reburied in the Bloemendaal honours field (No. 33).

They left behind a huge estate, and Elkan was its executor. Amongst all the beautiful treasures of the estate was a baroque clock, built around 1760 in Amsterdam. It is approximately three meters tall and made of burr walnut. Twelve old Dutch songs can be played, and it chimes low tones on the hour and higher tones on the half-hour. The hood is finished with fine filigree fretwork and a carved crest, crowned with a wooden Atlas figure and two wooden angels. Aunt Fie and Uncle Mau bought the clock at an auction and installed it in their luxurious house in a niche at the end of the long hallway. During the war, the butler entrusted the clock to a clockmaker, where it stayed in hiding until the end of the war.

In 1950, we had money to buy the clock out of Uncle Mau's estate because Elkan sold many resources that came to us after the war. The bank of Lippmann, Rosenthal, and Co. had been holding my father's shares in our family's business. These were returned to me, and Elkan was able to sell them but only for a fraction of their previous value. He also sold several houses that had belonged to members of my family who did not come back from the camps.

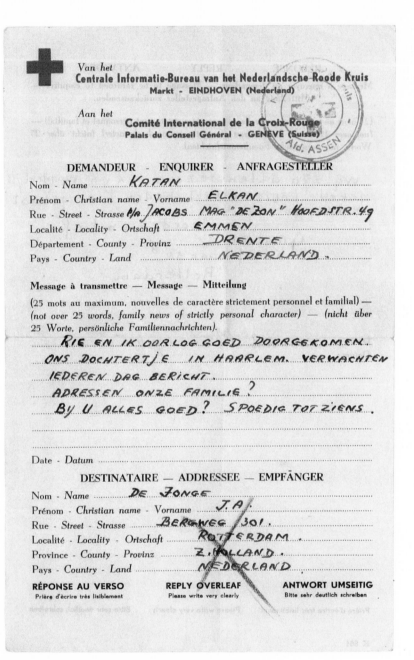

1945 - Another Red Cross form: Elkan looking for his mother.

CHAPTER 19

Keeping in Touch

We began to pick up the threads of our lives again. The paper work for Jeantje went through the court, again thanks to Mr. van de Bunt. He was Elkan's former employer who originally helped us get the false papers that made hiding Jeantje easier. We started all over again with our lives. We didn't have anything, but we were both very hard-working people.

But it was a desperately sad time for us because we found out what had happened to our families. The Red Cross posted a list of all the people who had been killed. There were so many beloved names on the list. It was terrible. We had lost almost all our friends and all our relatives. Nobody of my family, the van Daelens, came back. We had lost our whole world. How could we cope? How could Elkan concentrate on his work?

Everything was totally different. There were so few Jews left that the possibilities for visiting were minimal. Most of them lived in Amsterdam. Elkan thought it would be a good idea to start a new family right away. But I didn't think that would be a good idea. I thought we should wait at least a year until we were healthy enough. We needed to build up our lives first too. But I did plan on having a big family because now I was the only survivor of a large family. In 1947, our son was born and then came three more daughters, so we had five children. It took us at least ten years to create as normal a life as possible.

Of all my friends before the war, only one girlfriend, Lennie Schrammeyer, survived the war. She was a colleague from the pharmacy. It was she who looked after our treasures and returned them to us after the war. She lived in Den Brielle, and we always kept in touch. She started her own pharmacy there after the war, which was very courageous.

We also kept in touch with our new friends from the war. Jeantje always kept in touch with Papa and Mama Went and visited them many times. They loved her very much. Sadly, I think it was very difficult for Mama Went to give her little Anneke back to us. In 1947, she finally gave birth to a baby girl, and they named her Anneke. This did not work out very well for Jeantje, however, and somehow she never had a good relationship with the new Anneke. I think the new Anneke was always very jealous of the little girl who had come before her in the family.

1956 - Farewell for Peter Went as he immigrated to Canada. Left to right: Daan, Els, Peter, Dik, Aad, Joché, and Anneke.

1947 - Jeantje with the porcelaain-headed doll that had been a present from Papa Went for her 4th birthday.

The brothers still love Jeantje very much. They no longer call her Anneke, of course. In fact, right after the war, I decided to call her Jeanne, in memory of my twin sister, who was gassed in the ovens of Auschwitz. She was Jeanne from 1945 until the end of elementary school. But when she went to the Lyceum, she told me that she didn't feel at all like Jeanne. She wanted to call herself by her real name and that was Jochebed, and Joché, for short. And that name stuck.

Sadly, Mama Went died a few years after the war. All of the Went boys emigrated when they grew up. Peter, the third boy, went to Canada in 1956 and lives in Toronto. Dick moved to Switzerland. The third boy, Flip, went to Australia in 1955, and Joché has visited him there occasionally. In July of 1996, there was a huge Went family reunion in Switzerland and once more Joché felt that she was still their baby sister.

Joché continued to keep up a close and loving relationship with her nanny Martha Stol-de-Vries, until Martha died on 19 May 2008. Joché went back many, many times all through her childhood and adolescence to visit her, and they always loved each other very much.

The Went house named Woodbury, in Bloemendaal where Joché was in hiding.

I also kept in close touch with Fennie Schuitema, the daughter of the younger Schuitema family, who brought me the feminine napkins when I was in jail in Assen. After the war, Fennie got married, but her husband's health deteriorated in the 1960s and they had only a small income. As soon as Elkan and I could afford it financially, I gave Fennie substantial monthly support until her death.

In the 1970s, Fennie started to collect the colourful paper attached to teabags. She glued them most artistically on blank cards and sold them in order to earn some extra money. With the help of others, she collected thousands of these attractive teabag attachments. Of course we all bought her cards, and I still have a few of them. Fennie was a dear friend, and we continued to exchange news with her parents who had hidden us during the war. I shall never forget that pickled pig under the bed! Fennie's father, Sjoerd Schuitema, lived to be 96 years old; Fennie's mother passed away much earlier, in 1947, when she was 62. Along with Wessel and Fennie, they had eight other children.

Bep and Corrie van Seijen were also frequent visitors to our house in Scheveningen. Jan worked as a border commissioner in Drenthe and, in 1951, they moved to Maassluis, as Jan received a promotion in the Customs office. Jan and Bep had three daughters and a son: Corrie and Riekje were the only ones who lived through the war. After the war, Bep and Jan would not talk about that time. It was not until after Jan died in 1965 that Bep decided to tell her children some of the stories.

Later, after the war, all was totally different for us as Jews. It was customary for our family to be members of the Orthodox synagogue in Rotterdam, and I will be buried next to my husband in the Jewish cemetery in Wassenaar when the time comes. But I do not participate in synagogue life: After learning that my whole family was murdered, I lost all my faith and trust in religion. I cannot give these beliefs a place in my life anymore, but I will always keep my Jewish background and culture. I tried to pass on my feelings to my children, but not always successfully. I can see that my grandchildren will have "mixed" marriages. That, for my family, is different. That is something I now have to accept. I had a good life with Elkan, who provided for us very well. We had a happy marriage of 52 years until he passed away 24 October 1992 at the age of 80.

In the summer of 2005, just before my 90th birthday, it was very hot in the Netherlands, and the heat has always bothered me. Joché, my daughter, who was visiting from Canada, proposed that we take a drive up north and visit her friend, Margriet, who lives north of Drenthe. When we were close to our destination, we saw the signs: "To Westerbork Camp" and "To Westerbork Village." Joché asked me if I wanted to stop in to see the camp again, since we were so close. I agreed half-heartedly to look around the Remembrance Centre. It is a modern building, and I was hesitant to enter. However, I caught sight of a table with books for sale. I found the book "Uit de dood herrezen" (Return from Death) by Max Stad, who was a friend of mine from Rotterdam. Then the lady at the reception asked us if we wanted to visit the place where the camp used to be: The trolley was leaving in five minutes. My reply? "No, absolutely not. I have been there already." Is this my definitive memory of those tragic years? Not really. It was indeed a dreadful time when so many people all over the world wished the Jews dead. But the people who were good to us during and after the war remind me that there are many good people in Holland. It is Martha's words in her last letter to Jochebed in the diary that end my story.

Never forget what your foster parents have done for you. They have loved you as if you were their own child . We wish you nothing but happiness and wellbeing! Bye, bye, dear little Anneke. Thanks for the sunlight you have brought us in these difficult war years.

1995 - Mrs. Pepping and Rie

1995 - Aunt Martha and Joché in Velp.

AFTERWORD

My symbol of Freedom

My symbol of freedom is a tree,
Not any tree, a special tree,
A tree in Amsterdam,
A backyard chestnut tree.

Huge now, wide and high,
But small then more than sixty years ago.
Small too was the fourteen-year-old girl,
who watched the tree by night,
from her unlit window.

She saw its branches, its leaves,
And saw it blooming.
She watched the tree by night,
When there was light in the sky,
But never by day.

The seasons went by,
But she, she could not be seen,
She could not be free,
She could not …..

The tree is still there,
I saw it and loved it,
And wish Anne Frank could now see
This symbol of freedom.

Jochebed Katan, 1989.

Jochebed's Life after the War

Jochebed speaks:

In my youth, I was the only child in the family who was interested in hearing my mother's stories about the wartime. However, the subject was considered taboo in our home. Occasionally, keeping it a secret from my father, my mother told me about parts of her earlier life. She felt it was important for me to know a little bit about the story because I was her oldest daughter and because I was part of the war story. Looking back, I feel as though it was unfair of my father to prohibit my mother from openly speaking about the tremendous losses of her family members; while my father's siblings had all survived.

It wasn't until 1992, after my father's death, that the whole story was told. That evening, right after Elkan's funeral, my mother told all of her four remaining children and their partners the entire dramatic story. We had no tape recorder that night, but later, my mother and I recorded all her memories for her children and grandchildren.

I now know that my background is very unusual: I am a Dutch Jewish hidden child and a Holocaust survivor; as well, both my Jewish parents survived the Holocaust. While Tante Martha would have adopted me if my parents never came back, Papa Went always felt that I belonged in a Jewish household. There was no uncertainty about giving me back to my parents; however, this was not the case for many children. Many Dutch families wanted to keep the children they had hidden, especially if they were young. It was hard to give up these children they had come to love as their own. Usually, only one parent would return, and they would often be in poor physical and mental condition. In such a case, the Jewish agency had to mediate. If no parent came back, the Jewish agency would rule that the child needed to be placed with another Jewish family member or in a Jewish orphanage, no matter how happy the child was with their hiding family. It was certainly not always the case that a hidden child would see their rescuers again. My parents, however, were willing to allow me to visit the Wents many times and keep a good relationship with them. I feel a responsibility to record my observations about the effect this dual heritage has had on me and my life.

What was our life like after the war? For the first 5 years, we had a very difficult life. I begin with the "second big day in my life," as my Tante Martha describes it. I was the youngest of 7 children in the Went family—the beloved little baby sister. The boys had created a lively, interesting environment in which I thrived. Tante Martha, the nanny, showered me with love and attention. Papa Went adored me.

When my parents came back into my life, my whole world turned upside down. My Went brothers remember that I cried when my parents took me away from the Went home. Even as young as two years old, I had hated change. Tante Martha told how I cried when the furniture was moved out of the Went house when they were forced by the Nazis to move to another house. But, when my parents took me away from the Went home, my whole world changed: I was transported to a troubled world with no big brothers to make life fun, and my parents hardly knew the little girl I had become.

The unconditional love that I had experienced in the Went

family was gone, and there was no closeness between my parents and me. I often wondered why they could not be more loving towards me, considering that, of all my mother's loved ones, I was the only one who came back to them. After all, most Jewish children had been killed. Maybe they did not realize what a miracle it was that I survived? Very recently, in reading "Beyond Anne Frank" by Diane L. Wolf, I learned that most young Dutch Holocaust survivors had this same experience of not feeling loved by their parents. In fact, it seems that the parents' traumatic experiences made them incapable of giving love, even to their own children.

I know that both my parents had much to cope with after the war. They had to find a place to live, and my father had to re-establish himself in his career. My mother learned that family member after family member was not coming back because they had been gassed in the concentration camps. Most of their friends were killed, too. They even had trouble getting their belongings back from "friends." At the same time, they were renovating the house in Scheveningen, and my father, in addition to going back to work, had to deal with the large estate of Uncle Mau, which kept him very busy.

After the war, my mother wanted to have a large family. My brother, Nico, was born in 1947, Sonja in 1948, Hedie in 1951, and Eveline in 1954. Now I was the big sister. But each new birth could not erase the memories of those who had been taken from my mother and murdered. There was very little family life left, and it was all from my father's side of the family, where, miraculously, none had been killed. I had one grandmother, Oma Juul, but she passed away on December 31st, 1956, when I was thirteen years old. Aunt Eef, a beloved aunt, came every Friday night for dinner.

My parents had a great deal of pride, and our family always looked well cared for. We were nicely dressed and well fed. There was always pressure for us to excel at school. My parents wanted me to have Jewish friends, but there were hardly any left. Most of the Jewish children of my age had been killed or had emigrated to

Israel right after 1948; often, they were orphans. My siblings and my cousins were too young to be playmates. I was lonely.

I heard a story about Harry, a child survivor, who was born in 1943 [like me] in Amsterdam. He asked his father, "Why are there no other Jewish children to play with? Where are they all?" His father replied only, "Gone." Nothing was explained. I went through the same experience after the war.

I was one of the "lost" generation, and I have felt this way throughout my life. My siblings, born in the "baby boom," had lots of Jewish friends, but I did not.

Once, in elementary school, I was called a "dirty Jew" by a schoolmate, the son of the fish merchant. I felt attacked and started fighting with him. Even though he was much taller than me, I tore his shirt. My parents took care of the incident but did not talk to me or explain anything.

I never had a warm relationship with my father. After the war, he was busy reorganizing and rebuilding our lives, and his office in our house was completely off-limits to us children. The phone in the office and the extension in the living room were for the adults. My mother always said if we wanted to talk to our friends, we could take our bikes and go over to their houses. When clients came to see my father, we had to be very quiet, with our toys out of sight. My father became very bad tempered after the war, probably due to stress, and I came to fear his varying moods. He and I spoke only about the stock exchange, cars, and the weather. He was only able to show affection to one of my sisters.

The subject of the war was entirely taboo in our house. I never understood why I was not allowed to talk about the war with my father. Right after the liberation, my father decided that there was to be no discussion about the time before or during the war. Why would my father never allow my mother to speak about all her losses? I don't think he lost anyone in his immediate family. Unfortunately I never asked him.

He denied us all the opportunity to reflect upon the enormity of everything that had happened. He suppressed all thoughts and feelings about the past and entirely distanced himself from the experience. He threw himself into hard work, successfully building a new life for his family. In this way, he intended to protect his children from the terrible knowledge of the Holocaust. I think this was the way many Dutch people coped with the divisions within society after the war.

My parents assimilated into the new Dutch society but kept the Jewish traditions, such as Chanukkah, the High Holidays, and Pesach [Passover]. They found new Jewish friends. My father served on the Board of my Lyceum for many years. My mother never worked outside the home, just like before the war. She was busy looking after our family. She played tennis once again, and together they played bridge every Thursday night. They hired a maid and sent out the laundry to be washed.

I never talked with my non-Jewish friends about how I had been hidden as a baby with the Went family. Nor did I tell them that I really had two families as a result of this experience. I took for granted that I had another family who loved me, and I don't think I ever realized that that was unusual. Only Dr. Cardozo, a professor at my Teacher's College, ever asked me about my experiences during the war. He was a psychologist and was Jewish himself.

The Wents continue to be important to me today, and I visit them as often as I can. My "brothers" have been extremely helpful in remembering wartime stories for this book. Tante Martha left the Went family's employment upon her marriage to Ru Stol after the war, and they had four children: Marijke, Pauline, Liesbeth, and Peter. But she remained my beloved nanny until her death on May 19, 2008. There was always a special bond between Martha and me, and she always thought of me as her first baby.

I went to the holiday camps of the Jewish youth movement Habonim about three times a year, where I met Jewish children who had also been in hiding. They mainly came from Amsterdam, and many were orphans; I lost touch with them around the age of sixteen, because most of them moved to Israel. Also, I fell in love with a nice Gentile boy. My parents were very set against this relationship: First, he was not Jewish. Second, they thought he came from a more modest background. I had many quarrels with my parents.

When I was eighteen, they sent me to Israel for six weeks in the hope that I would change my mind about my boyfriend. I never told them that in Israel a German Gentile boy fell in love with me. He was there for one year to apologize to the state of Israel for his parents' actions as Nazis during the Holocaust. But I did not feel at home in Israel; I couldn't get used to the climate and the language. I decided not to emigrate to Israel, but instead to became a school teacher in Holland, which I had wanted to be all along. I went to Teacher's College for 4 years and became a teacher like my grandmother, Sara.

The more my parents set themselves against my relationship with my boyfriend, the more estranged I became from them, and the closer I became with him. In 1965, when I was 22 years old, we were married. The same year, I became an elementary school teacher.

My first husband and I have two children: A son, Hajo Adriaan (Papa Went's name) Jeroen, and a daughter, Marjoleine Anneke (my hiding name) Eva (my beloved aunt). Both of our children married and have children, giving me five grandchildren. My mother lived to see three of her great-grandchildren, who were her pride and joy.

We lived in a completely non-Jewish environment. I kept the Jewish part of my life secret and that had consequences. I always felt insecure in school, in larger groups, and later as an adult. Any time I was in a non-Jewish environment, I avoided talking about Judaism. Because of my experiences growing up, I felt that if people knew I was Jewish, they would treat me differently and perhaps reject me. Even after I emigrated to Canada, when people would ask, "Where does the name Jochebed come from?" I answer, "Oh, I am from Holland." When I started telling my story in schools, in my early 60s, I hesitated to write my full name on the blackboard. I overcame this because my story starts with my name. I have been named Jochebed, Jeantje, Julie van de Zomer, Anneke van Duin, and Joché. If I cannot talk about my name, the story has no beginning.

Now that I have recaptured so much more of the hidden part of my past, I feel so much more complete, and also I am much more able to talk about it to strangers. After doing all this research and writing it all down, I have become much less insecure. I've always said, "Once in hiding, always in hiding", but now I've been able, more or less, to overcome this.

I became more interested in Judaism as I grew a little older. Several times, I went to the Anne Frank House Museum in Amsterdam. I have always felt a deep connection with Anne, who was 14 years older than me, and who was in hiding so close to where I was born in Amsterdam. She was put on the very last train to leave Camp Westerbork; it is so sad to think that she almost survived.

My mother and I both donated money on behalf of our family to the Appelplatz Memorial at the Camp Westerbork Museum. This memorial is in the shape of a map of the Netherlands and is formed by 102,000 small rectangular stones. Each stone memorializes one person who was shipped to the concentration camps. The Jewish stones are topped with a silver Star of David. It is quite moving to see that each stone is different in height: The higher the stone, the older the person.

Author's Note: Today there is a memorial at Westerbork. A plaque with a quotation from Lamentations reads (translated):

"Men stalked us at every step,
so we could not walk in our streets.
Our end was near,
Our days were numbered,
For our end had come."

The rusting steel rails, still set on their worn ties and oil-stained gravel, run for about fifty meters from the middle of Camp Westerbork towards Germany. Then, their ends twist upwards and point to the sky.

I also became more interested in my parents' clock, which they had bought from Uncle Mau's estate. When my parents moved into a condominium where the ceilings were too low for the clock, my father gave the clock to me. Most other clocks like this are now in museums. I also began to appreciate my mother's beautiful china cups, the fish plates, and the silver cutlery, which had been hidden during the war. My grandmother had twelve beautiful teacups that she bought in 1920 at Jungerhans, a well-known specialty store in Rotterdam. Mrs. Bruinhout, in Schiebroek, hid the cups and the silver cutlery during the war. After the war, she returned the cups and the silver cutlery to my mother. The treasures survived but not the people . . .

It was when I emigrated to Canada in 1989 when I was 46 years old, that I began in earnest to explore my Jewish roots. My second husband was very interested in Judaism, so we joined a Reform Congregation in Kingston, Ontario. I am now part of a relaxed Jewish community. I have been learning about the services and the Torah. I have joined a Jewish choir and started a Jewish Women's Study Group, and my life is enriched, living in this community. I have made many good friends here in Kingston and many of them are Jewish.

My mother too has died now—thirteen years after my father. Rie was almost 90 when she passed away in the hospital in The

Hague on July 4th, 2005, just one week before her 90th Birthday. She was buried next to my father in the Jewish cemetery in Wassenaar. It was a rainy day, but at the moment the casket was being slowly lowered into the ground, the sun came out. We gave her a small extra memorial stone on her grave, with the text: In memory of her loving parents, Hendrik and Sara van Daelen-Doodewaard, her twin sister Jeanne, and her brothers Simon and Aat. During the war, they were all killed in the camps. Rie has always missed them very much.

Ten years ago, I was invited to tell my story to a grade 8 class in Napanee, ON. This was the beginning of many presentations. I have now been invited to tell my family's story to a variety of groups in the Kingston area: high school classes, mainly grades 10, 11 and 12; Queen's university students; Human Resources teachers; retired women; and the 2008 Yom Hashoah remembrance service for 300 people.

2006 - Elkan's and Rie's graves in Wassenaar. The extra stone is in memory of Rie's immediate family who were killed during the Holocaust.

Cobblestones at Camp Westerbork. Each one represents a life lost. The height of the stone indicates the age of the person: The taller, the older.

In 2008, I was approached by my friend, Pam Simon, who teaches Holocaust history to grade 10 students at QECVI, a local high school. She wanted to start a museum about the survivors living in Kingston; each of the eight survivors was invited to tell his or her story and write down significant events. Each of us had a cardboard tree decorated by one of the students, for which we provided the text, photos and other decorations related to our lives. For example, my tree had decorations of fish and seashells because of my grandmother's fish plates, which were hidden and then reclaimed—just like me.

Then I began to visit important places from my past. In April 2012, I went with my daughter Marjoleine to Amsterdam for a day. We went to the Hollandse Schouwburg at the Plantage Middellaan. This was the place from which my mother, father and I, with help from the German Alfons Zündler escaped in 1943. When I arrived at the information desk, there was a notice that donations were appreciated. The old man behind the desk who welcomed us was very surprised at my generous donation. I said "This is my donation, because I've been here already." The man was very helpful when I asked if he had photos from the wartime, and he gave me several. For instance, the photo of Mrs. Pimmenthal, the director of the daycare across from the Hollandse Schouwburg, was one that came from him. As the building had become derelict and had been raided for wood in the Hunger Winter the entire inside of the theatre was torn down after the war. It was turned into a memorial in 1958. There was an open square with a memorial covered in flowers, and the only parts of the building that were pre-war were the offices upstairs and the facade. It was very moving to see the glass wall at the entrance of the building: On this wall were engraved the 6700 family names of the Jews killed during the war. This was an amazing experience to share with my daughter, Marjoleine.

I have spent a great deal of time corresponding with the people who helped my parents during that dark time. In April 2012, I met Corrie van Seijen and her two sisters in The Hague. Corrie is the daughter of Bep and Jan, and she was the little girl who brought their dinners up to the attic every night and for whom my parents made the book for her 7th birthday. I didn't know Corrie's sisters well, but Corrie and I had grown very close through Skype conversations. Marjoleine was with me, and we both got very excited when we saw them coming. Seeing Corrie, I felt as if I was meeting a lost sister again. She hugged me very warmly. She brought several pictures from the war years, and I had a lot of questions about her parents and mine. We both felt sorry to be living so far apart. Corrie is as loving as her parents were.

In that same week, I met Lisa van de Bunt for the first time in my life. Lisa is the son of Mr. and Mrs. van de Bunt, who played a huge part in our survival. Mr. van de Bunt was my father's employer both before and after the war. Mrs. van de Bunt collected me and took me to the Went house when my parents had to give me up. They housed us and looked after us when the war was over, and continued to be good friends with my parents throughout their lives.

When I met Lisa at the station in Haarlem, near where he lived, he immediately said, "We are not going to my house. We are first going to Bloemendaal, to the house where you were in hiding." He drove to "Woodbury," still the name of the house where I had lived as a baby and toddler with the Went family. I recognized the house from the characteristic shape of the windows, which I had seen in photos. We walked up to the front door, and I saw, to my astonishment, the original nameplate with the name Went on it. We decided to ring the bell; the door was opened by Saskia Went, who is the wife of a cousin of my Went brothers. We were invited inside and saw that the house was being completely renovated. I didn't recognize anything, but I was very grateful to Lisa for taking me back to that house after 68 years.

Researching this book has been unexpectedly rewarding. My research began by sorting out all the materials and photos in the boxes I inherited from my mother. I felt a great urge and enthusiasm to archive it all. There were many things I did not know my mother had: She kept all the important documents, such as her identity card from Camp Westerbork. After two years of going through all these papers and reading 35 letters, I suddenly found an envelope containing the farewell letter from Jeanne, Rie's twin sister, and a very dear letter written to Rie from her mother Sara, at the time that I was born. These two letters from the two people my mother loved most were the most important letters she had ever received. I did not know my mother had saved these letters, so imagine how I felt when I found that envelope.

Only now, through writing this book, have I discovered what a wonderful family my mother had. I know much more about their characters and their lifestyle, and it is very sad that I could never meet them. In hindsight, I understand and am happy that I had the name Jeantje ('Little Jeanne') for so many years. It has been my responsibility and my honour to publish this story, along with my mother's documents and family photographs, in remembrance of her entire family, who were murdered by the Nazis during the Holocaust.

Jochebed Katan

APPENDIX A

van Daelen Family Tree

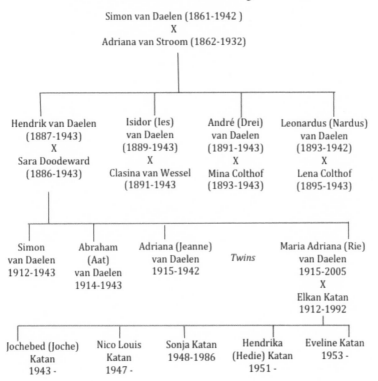

Simon van Daelen (1861-1942)
X
Adriana van Stroom (1862-1932)

Hendrik van Daelen
(1887-1943)
X
Sara Doodeward
(1886-1943)

Isidor (Ies)
van Daelen
(1889-1943)
X
Clasina van Wessel
(1891-1943

André (Drei)
van Daelen
(1891-1943)
X
Mina Colthof
(1893-1943)

Leonardus (Nardus)
van Daelen
(1893-1942)
X
Lena Colthof
(1895-1943)

Simon
van Daelen
1912-1943

Abraham
(Aat)
van Daelen
1914-1943

Adriana (Jeanne)
van Daelen
1915-1942

Twins

Maria Adriana (Rie)
van Daelen
1915-2005
X
Elkan Katan
1912-1992

Jochebed (Joche)
Katan
1943 -

Nico Louis
Katan
1947 -

Sonja Katan
1948-1986

Hendrika
(Hedie) Katan
1951 -

Eveline Katan
1953 -

Katan Family Tree

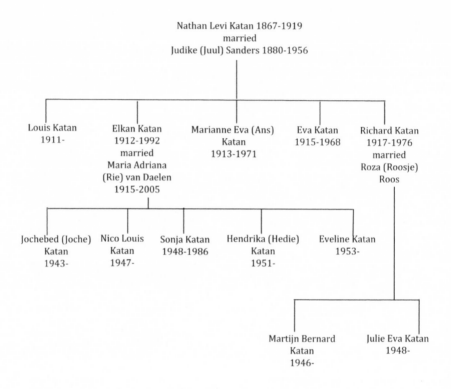

Nathan Levi Katan 1867-1919
married
Judike (Juul) Sanders 1880-1956

Louis Katan
1911-

Elkan Katan
1912-1992
married
Maria Adriana
(Rie) van Daelen
1915-2005

Marianne Eva (Ans)
Katan
1913-1971

Eva Katan
1915-1968

Richard Katan
1917-1976
married
Roza (Roosje)
Roos

Jochebed (Joche)
Katan
1943-

Nico Louis
Katan
1947-

Sonja Katan
1948-1986

Hendrika (Hedie)
Katan
1951-

Eveline Katan
1953-

Martijn Bernard
Katan
1946-

Julie Eva Katan
1948-

Went Family Tree*

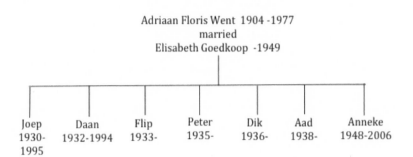

Adriaan Floris Went 1904 -1977
married
Elisabeth Goedkoop -1949

Joep	Daan	Flip	Peter	Dik	Aad	Anneke
1930-1995	1932-1994	1933-	1935-	1936-	1938-	1948-2006

*Nanny for the Went Family, and primary caregiver for
Anneke van Someren (Jochebed Katan) was:
Martha de Vries (Aunt Martha)
1917 - 2008

APPENDIX B

IN MEMORIAM

VAN DAELEN, HENDRIK (Rie's father), b. 2-6-1887 Vlaardingen, d. 11-6-1943, Sobibor.

VAN DAELEN- DOODEWAARD, SARA (Rie's mother), b. 2-2-1886 Rotterdam, d. 11-6-1943, Sobibor.

VAN DAELEN, SIMON (Rie's brother), b. 9-12-1912 Rotterdam, d. 30-4-1943, Sobibor.

VAN DAELEN, ABRAHAM DANIEL (Rie's brother Aat), b. 13-5-1914 Rotterdam, d. 28-2-1943, Auschwitz.

VAN DAELEN, ADRIANA (Rie's twin sister Jeanne), b. 10-7-1915 Rotterdam, d. 24-9-1942, Auschwitz.

VAN DAELEN-DE VRIES, ADELE (Rie's sister-in-law), b. 9-1-1915 Rotterdam, d. 19-10-1942, Auschwitz.

VAN DAELEN-WITSENHUIJSEN, ALICE (Rie's sister-in-law), b. 4-5-1917 Rotterdam, d. 30-4-1943, Sobibor.

VAN DAELEN, SIMON (Rie's grandfather fathers' side), b. 24-5-1861 Vlaardingen, d. 2-11-1942, Auschwitz.

VAN DAELEN-VAN STROOM ADRIANA (Jeanne) (Rie's grandmother fathers' side), b. 9-12-1862, d. 22-11-1932, Rotterdam.

DOODEWAARD, ABRAHAM DANIEL (Rie's grandfather mothers' side), b. 23-11-1859, d. 29-12-1920, Rotterdam.

DOODEWAARD-COHEN, ADRIANA (Rie's grandmother mothers' side), b. 18-1-1862 Dordrecht, d. 15-10-1942.

VAN DAELEN, DUIFJE (Rie's great-aunt), b. 14-5-1859, Vlaardingen, Netherlands, d. 19-10-1942, Auschwitz.

VAN DAELEN, ELISABETH (Rie's great-aunt), b. 31-12-1862, d. Vlaardingen,Netherlands, d. 15-10-1942, Auschwitz.

APPENDIX C

IN GRATITUDE

This is a list of people mentioned in the book who helped Rie, Elkan and Jochebed survive during the war. This list may not be complete.

In chronological order:

Lenie Schrammeyer, Rie's friend

Dr. van der Poort, the doctor who delivered Jochebed

The **young man in the birth registry office**, who did not turn the young family into the authorities

Alphons Zündler, the German official who accepted the bribe and allowed them to escape

Mr. J.A. Bruinhout, the friend who put Rie and Elkan in touch with the hiding network

The **Judge** who organized false papers for Jewish children

Mr. and Mrs. van de Bunt, who placed Jochebed with the Wents

The Went family, who welcomed Jochebed into their family

Tante Martha, Jochebed's nanny at the Went home

Elkan's young colleague who helped Rie and Elkan obtain false identity papers and accompanied them on the train

The Communists who forged their false identity papers

Jan, Bep and Corrie van Seijen, a hiding family

Fennie, Fenniechien and Sjoerd Schuitema, a hiding family

Wessel and Tina Schuitema, a hiding family

The Pepping Family, a hiding family

The Middel Family, a hiding family

The couple who hid Elkan in their cellar after Rie was rounded up

The Czech brothers who befriended Rie in Camp Westerbork and had the poster of her father's DeeWee product

Simon den Hartogh, Rie's cousin in Camp Westerbork who brought her a lock

The man who picked up Rie and her friends in his wagon on the road from Camp Westerbork

The lady who let Rie and her friends sleep in her haystack after their escape from Camp Westerbork and who fed them pancakes and eggs

The mixed marriage couple who let Rie and Elkan stay with them after Rie returned from Camp Westerbork

Those unknown to the author who helped Jochebed, Rie, and Elkan survive.

APPENDIX D

Legislation against the Jews in the Netherlands

This is a partial list.

1940

May 10: Beginning of the German occupation of the Netherlands.

September 14: Jews banned from markets in Amsterdam.

September 30: Circular to local authorities defining a Jew as anyone with one Jewish grandparent who had been a member of the Jewish community.

October 5: Civil servants forced to sign the "Aryan attestation."

October 27: Proclamation against the "Aryan attestation" read from many church pulpits

1941

January 10: Compulsory registration of all persons "wholly or largely of Jewish blood."

February 5: Doctors must declare if they are Jewish.

February 12: German authorities seal off the Jewish quarter in Amsterdam and insist on the establishment of a Jewish Council.

February 13: Establishment of the Amsterdam Jewish Council led by Professor David Cohen and Abraham Asscher.

April 11: First issue of the Joodsche Weekblad.

May 1: Ban on Jewish doctors, apothecaries, and translators working for non-Jews.

May 6: Designation of "Jewish streets" in Amsterdam.

May 31: Jews banned from using swimming pools and public parks and from renting rooms in certain resorts and coastal localities.

June 4: Freedom of movement of Jews restricted.

June 11: Raids of Jews in Amsterdam.

August 8-11: Regulations on the handling of Jewish assets and property. Registration of assets with Lippmann-Rosenthal Bank.

September 15: Signs reading "Forbidden for Jews" appear. Jews no longer allowed to visit parks, zoos, cafes, restaurants, hotels, guest houses, theatres, cabarets, cinemas, concerts, libraries, and reading rooms.

September 16: Travel permits introduced.

October 20: Jewish Council sanctions the creation of a card index of Jews in the Netherlands.

November 3: Jewish markets established in Amsterdam.

November 7: Jews banned from bridge, dance, and tennis clubs.

November 7: Jews banned from travelling or moving house without permission.

1942

January 1: Jews forbidden to employ non-Jewish domestic servants.

January 17: Beginning of the concentration of Jews in Amsterdam

January 20: Wannsee Conference in Berlin outlines practical measures for the extermination of European Jews.

January 23: Jews to carry identity cards with a letter "J".

April 24: Most Jewish butchers are closed.

May 1: Introduction of the Jewish Star for people and houses.

May 21: Jews forced to hand in all their assets and possessions valued at more than fl.250 to Llippmann-Rosenthal Bank by June 30th, 1942.

June 11-12: Jews banned from the fish-market. Jews no longer allowed to buy fruit and vegetables in non-Jewish shops. Bicycles and other vehicles ordered to be handed in.

July 1: SS takes over the supervision of Camp Westerbork

July 6: Jews no longer allowed to use telephones or visit non-Jews.

July 15: First trainload of Jews leaves Amsterdam. Deportations begin from Camp Westerbork to Auschwitz.

July 17: Jews allowed only to shop between 3:00 pm and 5:00 pm.

July 25: Prime Minister Gerbrandy urges help for the Jews via a broadcast from London on Radio-Oranje.

August: series of raids throughout the Netherlands. All Jewish street names changed.

September 16: First issue of exemption stamps from deportation to camps.

1943

April 23: The Dutch countryside declared free of Jews.

May 21: Jewish Council instructed to select 7,000 of its "exempt" staff for deportation.

May 26: Huge raids in Amsterdam to capture remaining Jews.

September 29: Jewish Council disbanded.

1944

May 16: Dolle Dinsdag. NSB leader Mussert orders the evacuation of Dutch National Socialists from the west and centre of the country to the east.

September 17: Operation Market Garden, the Allied airborne landings around Mijmegen and Arnhem, begins.

1945

May 5: Official liberation of the entire Netherlands.

Source: Moore, Bob, *Victims & Survivors: The Nazi Persecution of the Jews in the Netherlands 1940-1945*.

BIBLIOGRAPHY

Anderson, Anthony E. (1995 *Anne Frank was not alone: Holland and the Holocaust* [online]. Available: *http://www-lib.usc. edu/~anthonya/holo.htm Accessed 31/10/2011.*

Boas, Jacob, *Boulevard des Misères: The Story of Transit Camp Westerbork.* Hamden, Connecticut: Archon Books, 1985.

Blackburn, George G., *The Guns of Victory: A Soldier's Eye View*, Belgium, Holland, and Germany, 1944-45. Toronto: McClelland and Stewart Inc., 1996.

Foot, M.R.D., ed. *Holland at War Against Hitler: Anglo-Dutch relations 1940-45.* London and Portland, Oregon: Frank Cass and Company Ltd, 1990.

Greenberg, Irving. "The Righteous Rescuers". In Rittner and Myers, *The Courage to Care*, New York and London: New York University Press, 1986.

Hillesum, Etty, *Letters from Westerbork.* New York: Pantheon Books, 1986.

Hondius, Dienke, *Return: Holocaust Survivors and Dutch Antisemitism.* Trans. David Colmer. Westport, CT: Praeger, 2003.

Kasaboski, Tracy and den Hartog, Kristen, *The Occupied Garden: Recovering the Story of a Family in the War-torn Netherlands.* Toronto: McClelland & Stewart, 2008.

Law, Cecil E., *Kamp Westerbork: Transit Camp to Eternity: The Liberation Story.* Clementsport, N.S.: The Canadian Peacekeeping Press, 2000.

Maas, Walter B., *The Netherlands at War: 1940-1945*. London, New York and Toronto: Abelard, Schuman, 1970.

Moore, Bob, *Victims and Survivors: The Nazi Persecution of the Jews in the Netherlands 1940-1945*. London and New York: St. Martin's Press, Inc., 2007.

Paldiel, Mordecai, *Saving the Jews: Amazing Stories of Men and Women who Defied the "Final Solution."* Rockville, MD: Schreiber Publishing, 2000.

Rittner, Carol, RSM and Sondra Myers, eds, *The Courage to Care*. New York and London: New York University Press, 1986.

United States Holocaust Memorial Museum, "Key Dates." Holocaust Encyclopedia. http://www.ushmm.org/wlc/en/article. php?ModuleId=10007765. Accessed 31/10/2011.

United States Holocaust Memorial Museum, "Westerbork": Holocaust Encyclopedia. http://www.ushmm.org/wlc/en/article. php?ModuleId=10005217. Accessed 31/10/2011

Warmbrunn, Werner, *The Dutch under German Occupation, 1940-1945*. Stanford, CA: Stanford University Press, 1963.

Wolf, Diane L., *Beyond Anne Frank: Hidden Children and Postwar Families in Holland*. Berkeley and Los Angeles, CA: University of California Press, 2007.

Weber, Louis, ed., *The Holocaust Chronicle*. Lincolnwood, Illinois: Publications International Ltd., 2003.

Van der Zee, Henri A. *The Hunger Winter: Occupied Holland 1944-45*. Lincoln and London: University of Nebraska Press, 1982.

Vuijsje, Ies, *Tegen Beter Weten In*. Amsterdam: Augustus, 2006.

Zuehlke, Mark, *On to Victory: The Canadian Liberation of the Netherlands, March 23 – May 5, 1945*. Vancouver, Toronto, and Berkeley: D&M Publishers Inc., 2010.

If you would like to obtain one or more copies of this book, please send an email to:

jkatan.book@gmail.com

with your name and postal address.

Thank you,
Jochebed Katan